THE
ULTIMATE DROP

Too much to bear: a Hereford supporter after relegation is confirmed. (Photo: Tim Colville.)

THE
ULTIMATE DROP

George Rowland (ed.)

TEMPUS

First published 2001

PUBLISHED IN THE UNITED KINGDOM BY:

Tempus Publishing Ltd
The Mill, Brimscombe Port
Stroud, Gloucestershire GL5 2QG

PUBLISHED IN THE UNITED STATES OF AMERICA BY:

Tempus Publishing Inc.
2A Cumberland Street
Charleston, SC 29401

Tempus books are available in France and Germany from the following addresses:

Tempus Publishing Group   Tempus Publishing Group
21 Avenue de la République   Gustav-Adolf-Straße 3
37300 Joué-lès-Tours   99084 Erfurt
FRANCE   GERMANY

British Library Cataloguing in Publication Data.
A catalogue record for this book is available from the British Library.

ISBN 0 7524 2217 0

Typesetting and origination by Tempus Publishing.
PRINTED AND BOUND IN GREAT BRITAIN.

CONTENTS

ACKNOWLEDGEMENTS

There are numerous people whose help, support and knowledge of football have been invaluable in the production of this book. In addition to the individual contributors, I would like to particularly thank those mentioned below, without whom this venture may never have come to fruition:

Brighton & Hove Albion: Jackie Mooney, Tim Colville, Roy Scarborough (ROSCA); *Burnley:* Andrew Firmin, Brian Pim, Jane Pike, Andrew Hodson, Trevor Hodson, Ray Simpson, Edward Lee; *Carlisle United:* Dave Atkinson, Louise Porter; *Chester City:* Mark Davies, Neil Mullins, Scott Ingram, Dale Miles, Rob Ashcroft; *Colchester United:* Ray Cox, Ann Mills, Martin Strutt, Paul Ost, Andrew Cock, Elaine Soame; *Darlington:* John Ross, Ted Matthewson, Ted Blair, Steve Harland, John Hopps; *Doncaster Rovers:* Andrew Spiers, Shaun Flannery; *Hereford United:* Terry Goodwin, Chris Jones (Talking Bull), Peter Povall, Nigel Hill; *Halifax Town:* Adam Lee, Keith Middleton; *Lincoln City:* Phil Jarvis, Donald Nannestad; *Newport County:* David Hando, Chris West, Peter Stanford, Paul Cockerton, Ray Taylor, Chris Curtain, Richard Shepherd, Richard Crimmins; *Scarborough:* Wayne Fletcher, Helen Bart-Williams, Martyn Schwillens, Helen Mattingley, Dave Kettlewell.

Finally, I would like plug the following websites, many of which are run by those who have helped. Visit and enjoy!

> *www.kynson.org.uk* (Carlisle United - RIOA)
> *www.footie51.co.uk* (excellent general football site)
> *www. geocities.com/londonclarets/index.htm* (London Clarets - Burnley)
> *www. theimps.lincolnfans.co.uk* (The Forgotton Imps - Lincoln City)
> *www.albion-album.co.uk* (Tim Colville's Brighton photo pages)
> *www.imagesofpraise.com* (Dan Westwell's photography page)
> *www. Colchesterunited.net* (Colchester United Official Site)
> *www.burnleycisa.com* (Clarets Independent Supporters Association)
> *www. hufc.com/tb/index.htm* (Talking Bull - Hereford United)

DISCLAIMER

INTRODUCTION

There is little worse that can happen to one's team than relegation. The drop, demotion, the big fall; that terrible moment when it becomes mathematically impossible to escape the relegation zone and the dreaded 'R' appears next to your club's name when the league tables are shown on *Grandstand*. The maths are important. No matter how unlikely, how unfeasible it may be that a team may get the requisite points to survive, every fan clings on to the faintest hopes until the maths finally betray them. A miracle may happen and they may win their last four games, even though only two points have been won out of the previous eighteen. They could achieve the 6-0 away win at Gresty Road that will bring their goal difference to just the right level for survival. Until the maths are impossible, there is always a chance. Lucky pants, pre-match rituals, a last minute soul-selling deal with Beelzebub, they all offer hope until that fateful moment when the worst is confirmed, and the threat of the drop becomes a reality. Tax, death and relegation – all are inevitable. And for the fans of eleven League clubs it will happen this season – this much is guaranteed.

There is, of course, one demotion that surpasses them all. The biggest drop of all - the ultimate relegation. For the team that has the unfortunate distinction of finishing bottom of the Division Three, relegation not only means passage to a lower division, but a fundamental transition from a club with League status to non-League outfit. Essentially, there is little difference between the Rochdales, Wrexhams and Brentfords of the footballing world and the Stevenages, Worthings and Kingstonians. Certainly in terms of footballing quality there is precious little difference, as is demonstrated by the fact that no club promoted from the Conference has gone straight back down. Only Scarborough have returned whence they came, and thirteen years separated their promotion to, and relegation from, the League.

The difference between Division Three and the Nationwide Conference is a lot deeper than simply a question of footballing standards. It's a matter of status, of club pride and about ranking amongst one's peers. Leaving the League fold marks a departure from a brotherhood that includes illustrious names such as Liverpool, Manchester United and Arsenal to an allegiance with Hitchin Town, Nuneaton Borough and Northwich Victoria; automatic entry to the FA Cup proper is taken away and replaced by the FA Trophy and the Endsleigh Cup; removal of the League emblem from the letterhead of the club and the shirtsleeves of the players. It's about pride in one's club, and that above all is what matters most to a football fan. Pride is why League to Conference relegation will always be a far bigger drop than from Division Two to Division Three. And pride is what makes this relegation the bitterest pill of all for any football fan to swallow.

Finishing bottom of the League has not always had such fateful consequences. Until 1986/87, there was no automatic relegation from the Third (or Fourth as it then was) Division. The team that finished bottom of the pack had a safety net, in the form of re-election, and almost always this safety net held firm.

The system of re-election was about as unsporting as any dreamt up. The teams finishing in the bottom four of the old Fourth Division had to apply to the other League clubs and associate members for the right to remain in the League for another year. In almost all cases this application was successful and status was maintained. Having to apply for re-election held few fears. Imagine an exclusive Old Boys club being asked to decide on whether they should allow an old friend of years standing to remain a member, or whether they should exclude him to be replaced by a stranger with whom they have never had any connection. Combine this with the possibility that, come the next few years, any one of the voters could, in theory, find themselves in the same position, and facing the wrath of members they have previously voted against. The result is almost inevitable and the overwhelming desire to maintain the status quo meant that most wooden-spoon winners were given another chance. Granted, it was unfair to the clubs knocking at the door, begging bowl in hand, but vested interests were at stake. Of the 111 applications for re-election to the League since the Second World War, only 5 resulted in failure and expulsion from the League.

Football in its purest sense is a meritocratic system. If one club proves itself good enough on the basis of incontrovertible results over a season, it gains the right to progress through promotion to a higher level. In the same way if you finish bottom of the pile you relinquish your right to play in that division, and are obliged to take your place in the next lowest division for the following year. The system of election and re-election betrayed this principle of fairness. By the late 1970s, pressure was growing from aspiring non-League clubs for the system to be overhauled, and for some form of automatic promotion and relegation to the League to be instated.

In 1979, the non-League structure underwent a major overhaul. The sprawling leagues that had existed previously was replaced by a clear pyramid structure, with the Alliance Premier Division (later the Gola League, Vauxhall Conference and currently the Nationwide Conference) at the pinnacle – a clear top-flight of non-League football. The pyramid system meant that all non-League clubs, however lowly, had a direct path to the incontrovertible claim to be the champions of non-League football. The local village Miner's Welfare team could, following fourteen seasons of automatic promotion and a championship season, claim the title of

England's non-League champions. The way was open to all. And with the title came the strongest claim yet that the obvious reward should follow – automatic promotion to the Football League. The agenda was clear and the pressure and will from the non-League clubs relentless.

But still League membership for the champions proved an elusive goal. In the first seven years no club from the Alliance Premier was successfully elected to the League, and, barring Altrincham, who missed out in 1980 by one vote, none came close. It was clear that automatic promotion was the only way in which the rightful prize for the triumphant club could be ensured. In 1986 the Football League finally succumbed to the inevitable, and, provided that the non-League champions could demonstrate that they met stadium, financial and structural requirements, automatic relegation and promotion from and to the League was instituted.

Since 1987, nine clubs have made the ultimate step down into the Conference. Others have been more fortunate. The untimely demise of Aldershot and the increase in the size of the Football League meant a reprieve for Wrexham and Carlisle, bottom in 1991 and '92 respectively. Northampton, Exeter and Torquay escaped the drop due to the failure of Kidderminster, Macclesfield and Stevenage to meet the League's stringent stadium requirements and thus being denied progression (temporarily in the first two cases). Of the nine clubs, four have returned to the League fold. Lincoln City, the first club to be relegated to non-League football, returned after only one year, a feat repeated by Darlington in 1990. Colchester took two years to return by winning the Conference in 1992, whilst Halifax were promoted back to Division Three in 1998 after five years in the wilderness. Doncaster, Chester, Hereford and Scarborough (themselves the first beneficiaries of automatic promotion) remain in the Conference, whilst Newport County went out of business shortly into their first conference season, to re-emerge two divisions below as Newport AFC.

This book follows the fates of these nine clubs as they made their journey into the unknown territories of non-League football, as well as three clubs who have made 'great escapes' from the jaws of the ultimate relegation. In most cases the perspective is that of those to whom it means most of all – the fans, those individuals who have faced the abyss, not knowing whether they were ever destined to return. It chronicles the falls and rises, the relegations and promotions, financial woes, boardroom tussles, and a myriad of other circumstances that led to what, in footballing terms, must be considered the greatest relegation of all: the Ultimate Drop.

George Rowland
April 2001

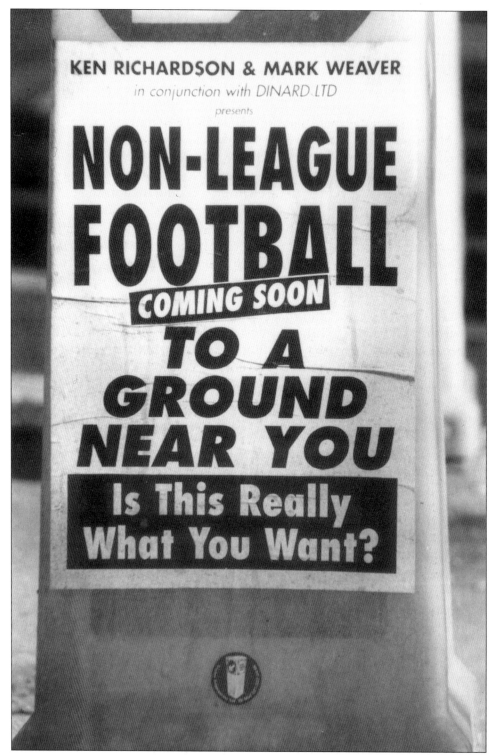

Doncaster fans' anti-Richardson poster. (Photo: Ray Gilbert.)

To 'Do a Lincoln'

George Rowland

1986/87   Bottom of Division Four, relegated to Conference
1987/88   Conference Champions, promoted back to Division Four
2000/01   Eighteenth in Division Three

In August 1986 the clubs of the Fourth Division embarked on a journey into the unknown. Automatic relegation from the League, much talked about in the past few years, had finally been introduced, and a one-way ticket to the Conference was the new prize for the bottom club. No longer was the League's basement fitted with the added safety net of re-election; the stakes had been raised, and trips to such football Meccas as Fisher Athletic, Enfield and Welling were in store for the losers. Prophets of doom were already decided on the fate of the unlucky club. Once relegated, they would be sucked into the quagmire of non-League football, and, unless they had already gone bankrupt, they would forever be consigned to life outside the League, never to return. It was an unknown quantity, and a new challenge to which no-one wanted to subscribe.

Pre-season favourites for the drop were undoubtedly Torquay United. Wooden-spoon winners for the past two seasons, Torquay were plagued by internal troubles that made most bookies offer longer odds on Christmas falling on 25 December than on Torquay avoiding relegation. Other likely candidates, Halifax and Rochdale, were never far from the foot of the League and so had to be in the frame. Preston North End and Cambridge finished second and third from bottom respectively in the preceding season, and so needed a significant upturn if they weren't to avoid the end-of-season dogfight. Exeter, Tranmere, and Peterborough were also mooted as possible victims of the new legislation. But the uncoveted title of first club automatically relegated from the League would go to none of these. On 10 May it was the fans of Lincoln City who were waking up to the prospect of Conference football, wondering where it had all gone wrong, and how, when the odds had seemed so much in their favour, they had been the ones to succumb.

It had been Lincoln's first season in the Fourth Division for five years, having been relegated from the Third the season before. To their fans it was only a temporary blip – Lincoln weren't a Fourth Division club. Granted they weren't a Second Division club either, but recent history had shown them more than capable of holding their own in the Third. It wasn't just the

Lincoln City embark on their fateful season in the Fourth Division. (Photo: Alan Wilson.)

Imps' fans who were of the opinion that their foray to the lower echelons of the League would be short. With one bookie, Lincoln were not only favourites for promotion, but for the Fourth Division title itself, pipping Wolves into second place. At the very least they could expect a higher mid-table finish, consolidation, and then a push for promotion the year after. Never was the possibility of exiting the division downwards even dreamt of.

The past few years had not been easy ones for the club. The 1984/85 season had ended with Lincoln being 'the other team' at Valley Parade on the day of the Bradford fire. Fifty-six people, two of them from Lincoln, had lost their lives on a day that was supposed to have been one of celebration for newly-promoted Bradford City. Football became an irrelevance as fans and players alike witnessed one of the worst disasters to hit English football. Four weeks later and disaster almost hit the Lincoln players themselves, when a plane on which they were travelling crash-landed at Leeds-Bradford airport, forcing an emergency escape. Pre-season training was the last thing on the players' minds in the summer of 1985, and their football inevitably suffered the following season.

1985 also saw significant changes in personnel at Sincil Bank, changes which were to have a fundamental effect on Lincoln's path over the next few years. March saw the resignation of chairman Dennis Houlston, to be replaced by John Reames. By his own admission, Reames was inexperienced in running a football club. Having only been on the Lincoln board of directors for a little over two years, he had been thrust onto the throne as the only candidate with the necessary finances to fulfill the role. Reames' board had a similar lack of experience, and this was to show in key decisions over the next two seasons.

Manager Colin Murphy's six-year reign also came to end at the end of the 1984/85 season, 'by mutual consent'. Finding a replacement proved less than an easy task for the fledgling board and, despite numerous names being linked to the job, it was not until shortly before the new season that John Pickering was confirmed in the post. This left precious little time for him to construct a team, and to find replacements for the summer departures.

Despite the summer turmoil, the season started well, with Lincoln rising to sixth after eleven games. However, cracks in the hastily assembled squad were soon to show. A run of ten defeats in eleven games by December saw their position plummet, and the end of Pickering's brief reign as manager. His replacement, George Kerr, was unable to stop the rot and by the end of the season Lincoln occupied twenty-first place in the Third Division. A season in the League's basement beckoned.

George Kerr set about strengthening the squad during the pre-season, bringing in old hands from his former club Rotherham, as well as a number of players from north of the border. The season started well, with the club losing only two out of their first eight games. By November they were established with the pack as promotion contenders and looking decidedly healthy. With the dawn of the New Year, Lincoln were comfortably positioned in seventh, with sights firmly set on at least a play-off place, if not automatic promotion itself. However, 1986 saw a significant and disastrous turn-around in the Imps' fortunes. Five consecutive defeats – in which Lincoln failed to score a goal – saw them plummet down the table. The poor form continued. Three games and two defeats later, patience with Kerr had run out. With City now eighteenth, the board unanimously voted to end his brief tenure.

Given that the end of the season was less than two months away, there was little time for the board to deliberate on Kerr's successor. However, the appointment that was made must have raised more than a few eyebrows. Given Lincoln's recent form, and the fact that the stakes were so high, one would perhaps have expected the vote to go to a well-seasoned manager, with significant experience at guiding teams through difficult times and bringing them out safely at the other side. This was not to be. The job of stopping the rot, and securing Lincoln's League status, was given to a man with precisely no previous managerial experience – midfielder Peter Daniel. Furthermore, Daniel was expected to fulfill this new role in the capacity of player-manager, with a double burden on his shoulders. It was an appointment that Reames was soon to seriously regret.

The poor form continued. However, as late as 18 April, Lincoln still had five teams below them, and the odds were distinctly in their favour. By the start of May this had been reduced to three teams, but with three games to go, they required one single point to guarantee survival. A draw in any one of their last three games – away to Wolves, at home to Scunthorpe, or in the final match at Swansea was all that was needed. Even if the point didn't come, three other teams had to leapfrog the Imps for the worst to happen. They were firmly in the driving seat, and few in Lincoln were losing too much sleep.

Bottom of Fourth Division, 18 April 1987

	P	W	D	L	F	A	Pts
Lincoln City	**41**	**11**	**12**	**18**	**41**	**56**	**45**
Tranmere Rovers	40	10	14	16	49	64	44
Stockport County	39	11	10	18	47	65	44
Torquay	40	8	16	16	47	63	40
Burnley	40	10	12	18	48	68	42
Rochdale	39	7	16	16	41	64	37

Within ninety seconds of the trip to Wolves, Lincoln were playing catch-up. Steve Bull opened the scoring, and there was never any return for the Imps, who eventually lost 3-0. The Scunthorpe game was a different matter. With only eight minutes remaining, Lincoln were ahead by a single goal. Three points looked certain, when only the one was needed. However,

The slide continues with defeat against Cardiff on 7 February – midway through five straight defeats. (Photo: Alan Wilson.)

Just one point needed – goalmouth action against Scunthorpe. (Photo: Alan Wilson.)

in spectacular fashion, Lincoln not only threw away the lead in the last eight minutes, but also conspired to let in a second. From 1-0 up they finished the game 2-1 down, and still needing the elusive point for safety.

In the meantime, two other relegation candidates had pulled themselves clear of danger. Rochdale triumphed at Stockport on the last Wednesday of the season to ensure their safety and, two days later, Tranmere defeated Exeter to confirm their survival. It was all to come down to the last day of the season, with one of three teams doomed to the drop.

In the red corner were Lincoln – still favourites to escape – lying third off bottom with 48 points. A draw or win at Swansea or a defeat for either Burnley or Torquay would guarantee survival. In the blue corner were Torquay United, second bottom at start of play with 47 points. A win would buy them another year of League football, as would a defeat for Burnley or a draw with Lincoln losing. Finally, in the claret and blue corner were Burnley, rooted to the bottom on 46 points, and entertaining Leyton Orient, against whom they needed to win and hope that others tripped up.

Media attention focused intently on Burnley in the run-up to the big day. The papers were full of the 'big club fallen on hard times' stories. Saturday's *Football Focus* never even mentioned Lincoln in their build up. A crowd of over 16,000 crammed into Turf Moor, some of them ghoulishly hoping to see a glory club of yesteryear humiliated. The swelled crowd meant that kick-off had to be delayed by fifteen minutes, so that all could enter the ground. Once underway, the Clarets quickly took a 2-0 lead. Burnley were doing all they could to stave off the drop, and whilst the score at Turf Moor remained the same, their survival would depend on others' results. Torquay meanwhile were not finding the going so easy. Crewe had taken a 2-0 lead with a certain David Platt registering on the scoresheet. If all remained the same, they would be the fall guys.

Lincoln's match was a dire affair. With all to play for, the Imps couldn't raise their game, and by half time had gifted Swansea a two-goal lead. Ears were firmly fixed on the radio. Into the second half, news came in that Orient had pulled a goal back against Burnley. More important was the news that Torquay had also pulled one back against Crewe. Lincoln were still staying up, but it was getting tighter.

With only seven minutes remaining at Torquay, the Fates deemed it necessary to take a hand. The Gulls' full-back, McNichol, cleared the ball upfield, and in doing so stumbled onto the perimeter track. At that precise moment, PC John Harris happened to be circling the pitch with his police dog, Bryn. At the sight of the approaching McNichol, Bryn sprung into action. Fearing that his handler was about to be assaulted, he lunged at the defender and promptly landed a bite in his groin. McNichol collapsed in agony, and the match was halted for a full seven minutes whilst treatment was given.

Consequently, when the game at the Vetch Field finally petered out to a 2-0 defeat, both of the other crunch matches were still playing. Torquay's manager, on hearing the result from Swansea, was able to inform his players that all they needed was a single goal to survive. The Gulls launched a full on attack on the Crewe goalmouth. With only two minutes remaining the inevitable happened. Paul Dobson of Torquay seized on a mistake by a Crewe defender, steadied himself, and then bulleted the ball home, instantly becoming the hero of the South Coast club. The final whistle sounded and Torquay were safe. Burnley's match had finished with a 2-1 victory and they too were secure. Fifteen minutes after Lincoln's season had ended, they found themselves bottom for the first time and out of the League.

In any other season since the Fourth Division was established, Lincoln's record would have been sufficient to keep them off the bottom spot. Indeed, Lincoln had the highest points total of any team to finish bottom of any Football League division since before the war (even after adjusting to three points for a win). This was little solace to the Sincil Bank faithful. The town of Lincoln was in a state of shock. Instead of the expected promotion parties, they were experiencing relegation wakes. A combination of under-investment in the team, mediocre performances, and the farcical events at Plainmoor had resulted in seventy-five years of League football coming to an end.

In retrospect, Reames and his three-man board were brutally honest about their roles in Lincoln's disastrous two seasons. As board member Geoff Davey admitted, 'In our first years as a board we made some terrible,

terrible decisions.' Lincoln had been run as a business, and not as a football team. Reames had been financially very successful – Lincoln had ended both of his seasons at the helm in healthy profit. However, he had learnt the hard way that financial prudence does not buy success on the football field. A significant change in approach was necessary if Lincoln were going to bounce back quickly, and Reames knew it. An announcement was made that for the coming season Lincoln would maintain their fully professional status. Wages would be maintained at the Fourth Division level, in order to attract League quality players to Sincil Bank, and there would be significant monies made available for strengthening the squad. The lessons of two years of under-investment had been learnt and would not be repeated in the attempt to get out of the Conference at the first possible opportunity.

Relegation saw Daniel's brief reign as manager come to an abrupt end. His managerial record reads badly – played 14, won 2, drawn 5, lost 7 – and his club's League status. Over 120 applications were received for the vacant post, including submissions from such illustrious names as Alex Stepney, Trevor Cherry and Martin O'Neil. However, it was decided that for the task of resurrecting Lincoln City FC the job should go to the man who perhaps understood Lincoln's recent history better than anyone else. A man whose commitment to Lincoln could not be questioned and who undoubtedly felt the drive of regaining League status as much as the fans: Colin Murphy.

The news of Murphy's return was greeted with almost unanimous approval from the Lincoln fans. The whole city was lifted and everyone felt that a swift return to the League for the 1988/89 season was now a realistic possibility. The headline from the local paper 'Murphy's Mission' captured everyone's imagination and the black cloud that had descended over Lincoln began to dissipate. Murphy was always popular amongst the fans and the general feeling was that he was a manager who could give Lincoln City back its pride.

Murphy's task was immense. Due to an oversight on the part

Imps' Saviour – Colin Murphy. (Photo: Lincolnshire Echo.)

of the Football League, it became apparent that the players' contracts were no longer valid as Lincoln had now left the League fold. Consequently, all of the squad effectively became free agents, and had until 15 July to find themselves a new club. Unsurprisingly, a mass exodus followed and only four squad members, Nicholson, Buckley, McGinley and Gamble, decided to remain. Exactly five weeks separated the deadline for players to leave the club and the start of the Conference season – five weeks in which Murphy not only had to recruit the personnel for the coming season, but to also craft them into some sort of team.

The first match of the season came around all too quickly. Activity in the transfer market was frenetic: players were bought and thrust into the side within days, even hours of arriving. The first seven matches saw twelve debutants turn out for the Imps with hardly a chance to meet their colleagues, let alone get an understanding of their footballing qualities. Weymouth and Barnet were Lincoln's first opponents, and were able to take advantage of the ill-prepared opposition. After two games, Lincoln found themselves bottom of yet another division, having conceded seven goals. The long-suffering fans could be forgiven for despairing and wondering what the future had in store for their beloved side.

But it soon became clear that Murphy's Imps were not the lacklustre outfit that had apologetically finished the previous campaign. Murphy was putting together a side of battlers, a team who played with spirit and pride, and whose commitment was not in question. Fortunes quickly changed

Action from the final conference match v. Wycombe Wanderers. (Photo: Lincolnshire Echo.)

Champagne time! (Photo: Lincolnshire Echo.)

and, by October, Lincoln had established themselves in the promotion race. Their major rivals for the coveted spot were to be Barnet, managed by the effervescent Barry Fry. When the teams met at Sincil Bank on 28 October, tensions spilled over with on-field brawls seeing two players sent off and Barry Fry being escorted from the pitch. Even Reames and Davey got involved. Lincoln emerged 2-1 victors, but the promotion battle between the two clubs took on an extra edge.

Between December and April, Lincoln put together a sixteen-match unbeaten run, including a gratifying 5-1 drubbing of local rivals Boston United. A new Conference record attendance was set at that match with over 7,500 packing Sincil Bank. By the end of April, the Imps were one point behind Barnet, with two home games remaining. Yet again, they had to rely on results elsewhere.

The final Saturday of the season saw Lincoln entertaining Stafford Rangers in their penultimate game, whilst Barnet faced Runcorn. This time, the fates proved to be kind to Lincoln. Goals from Phil Brown and Clive Evans ensured three points for the Imps, whilst Barnet went down 2-1 to Runcorn. Lincoln topped the table for the first time, and, provided they could beat Wycombe Wanderers on the following Monday, they were guaranteed a swift return to the League.

Yet another Conference attendance record was set for the match against Wycombe, with 9,432 – Lincoln's largest crowd for over five years – cheering on the Imps. In the 22nd minute of the game Mark Setori scored the goal that the crowd had been waiting for. Tensions were relieved a little, but no-one was counting their chickens after events of recent years. But this time, nothing was to go wrong. Phil Brown scored a second goal in the 62nd minute and Lincoln held on for a comfortable win. The crowd erupted at the final whistle. Twelve months after the lowest point in their history, Lincoln had won the Conference and regained their place in the Football League.

The club that emerged from the Conference was in a far healthier state than the one which had entered it a year before. Crowds were at a five-year high on the back of Lincoln's first championship season in twelve years. The St Andrew's Stand had been officially opened, rejuvenating Sincil Bank and giving the outward appearance of a club investing in the future. The team was stronger and more settled than it had been in years, and under Murphy's leadership were expected to be a force in the Fourth Division the following year. The general consensus of opinion was that relegation from the League had been the necessary shot in the arm for a club stagnating under an unambitious and overcautious board. Lincoln had proved the doubters wrong. Relegation from the League was not necessarily a one-way ticket into oblivion. Lincoln had shown the way to the clubs who would later suffer the same fate. From now on, the League's fall guys would be looking to 'do a Lincoln', and emerge from the Conference at the first attempt.

Fans celebrate the return to the League. (Photo: Lincolnshire Echo.)

The joy after the despair. (Photo: Lincolnshire Echo.)

CLARET AND VERY BLUE (BURNLEY)

Igor Wowk, Andrew Hodson and Tony Scholes

1986/87 - Escaped relegation to Conference on final day of season
2000/01 - Seventh in Division One

The present day Burnley team has one thing in common with its 1987 counterparts: there's a real chance that they soon could be out of the Football League. The difference is, this time they're looking to move in an upward direction into the Premiership. Fourteen years ago, they almost left through the trap-door into non-League oblivion. At kick-off time on 9 May 1987, Burnley were bottom of Division Four and ninety minutes away from Conference football – that's how close it came. Thank God that's where the similarities end.

Burnley's decline had been slowly gathering momentum over the previous decade. A last shot at life in the First Division after the Second Division championship in 1972/73 had paved the way for three seasons of top-flight football at Burnley, ending in relegation in 1976. Jimmy Adamson's boast that Burnley would be 'The team of the seventies' proved to be hot air and the fans realised that after this relegation, there would be no quick return to the big time.

Further heartache followed quickly when, in 1979/80, the club fell into the Third Division for the first time in its history. A brief respite of promotion in 1981/82 couldn't stop the downward spiral and the club sank into the basement division, at the end of the 1984/85 season. For many diehard Clarets, this was the ultimate disaster. If only they knew how bad it would get.

The disastrous appointment of John Bond in 1983 greatly contributed to the problems that were to follow. He sold players that would 'obviously' never make it in the game (such as Lee Dixon), replacing them with expensive journeymen such as Gerry Gow, Tommy Hutchison, Steve Daley and Kevin Reeves at highly inflated wages. Bond was a disaster for the Clarets and most Burnley fans will never forgive him for what he did to our club in only fourteen months. The damage was to prove nearly terminal.

By 1986, the club was at its lowest ebb financially. At the start of the season they were £800,000 in debt and losing £10,000 a week. Pre-season, the club chairman had to go cap-in-hand to the TSB. One of the conditions they imposed for continued financial help was the withdrawal of the reserve side from the Central League. As Newcastle were to find out in later years, the absence of a competitive arena for the second string is a blow for any football club. It was to prove a further bodyblow for an already weakened set-up at Turf Moor.

Supporters were asked to buy shares in a rights issue, at £15 per share, as the club desperately hung on. For a while it looked as though any contributions would be money down the drain as there was no positive news, in fact no news at all from Teasdale. 'He's going to end this club,' said *Lancashire Evening Telegraph* reporter Keith McNee, 'I'll never forgive him.' Eventually share certificates were issued and support was given by the bank for another season. All in all, the situation was more than dire. It's difficult to conceive how the club managed to survive to the healthy state of today; it could so easily have simply folded.

Frank Teasdale had taken over the year before as chairman from Mr Jackson. For those that give Teasdale stick about his parsimony and thrift, they would do well to look at the set of circumstances he inherited. Apart from the financial disarray, the club had gone through two managers in his first season when Martin Buchan suddenly realised that club management was a bit different from going up for the toss every week for Manchester United. For the rest of the season the side had been managed by Tom Cavanagh, brought in by Buchan initially to help with pre-season training. However, on 30 June Cavanagh quit on medical grounds, and on 1 July Brian Miller was prised away from his Worsthorne newsagents and

Frank Teasdale. (Photo: Burnley Express.)

Brian Miller.

put in charge of the club for the 1986/87 season. Speculation had centred around the return of Martin Dobson (as was usual at the time), but he scotched all rumours by signing a three-year contract with Third Division Bury. Ironically, Miller stated his objective as getting out of the Fourth Division and back into the Third. As we all know, Brian nearly kept the first part of his pledge, but not the latter.

The previous season had seen the side finish a disappointing fourteenth. This was the last season of four up and four down automatic promotion and relegation, and the new play-off system was introduced, although not in its present format, as one of the bottom sides from the division above was also involved. More controversially, the concept of re-election to the Fourth was abandoned and relegation to the GM Vauxhall Conference for the last placed club was introduced – although no mention of this appears in the club magazines at the start of the season, as it couldn't happen to us, could it?

The close season activities were not very encouraging. Alan Taylor, top scorer with 16 goals in 1985/86, joined Bury; Vince Overson joined John Bond's Birmingham for £20,000 (who says he never did a good deal?);

Kevin Hird, joint second top scorer with Neil Grewcock (7 goals), joined Colne Dynamoes and Les Lawrence, with 6 goals in 16 starts the previous season, joined Peterborough on a free. Additionally, Peter Devine broke his leg whilst on holiday, never to play for the Clarets again, and five youth players were released, including England youth cap Andy Kilner (later to re-emerge briefly with Stockport County).

At one point Miller had only thirteen full-time professional players. This included Steve Kennedy, who retired during 1986/87 through injury, and Jim Heggarty, who cancelled his contract shortly after the start of the season. Furthermore, due to his dubious medical condition, Gallagher had not made any League appearances in 1985/86. Miller boosted his squad by adding Leighton James and Billy Rodaway prior to the start of the new campaign. The lack of continuity in the side is emphasised by the fact that at the start of the season only three players had made more than fifty appearances for the club: Hampton (83), Grewcock (80) and Malley (52), not counting the extensive Burnley careers of the returning James and Rodaway. So the scene was set. Looking back at the combination of these circumstances gives you some flavour of the 'challenge' Miller took on.

Despite the loss of key players, the Clarets made a reasonable start to the season. On the first day they took a point from the long trek to Torquay. They also squeezed a draw in the first leg away to Rochdale in the Littlewoods Cup, and followed this with a home victory versus Scunthorpe. We even seemed to shake off the ignominy of Rochdale cruising through in the second leg at the Turf 3-1.

Things were going fairly well in the League, and the Clarets managed a particularly fine 1-0 win at Wolves, with Grewcock scoring to complete a rare away victory at Molineux. The 3-0 win over Halifax took the Clarets to fifth place in late September. However, defeats away to Tranmere, and a 4-1 walloping at home to a rampant Preston North End soon brought us down to earth, and henceforward the season declined sharply. From this point we never saw the top half of the division again.

The month of October was disastrous, as only a home victory against Stockport punctuated the thrashings. A 0-0 home draw at the beginning of November brought about an almost complete collapse of support, as only 1,692 – the lowest post-war crowd for a League match – turned out in midweek to see the Clarets stem the tide by beating Colchester 2-1. I have often thought that a medal ought to be struck for those 1,692, for they are the real die-hards and in a way the rest of us are just 'bandwaggoners'. What a God-awful sight it must have been emerging from the tunnel on that night, and seeing so few bothered to turn out to watch you 'entertain.' If that's not confidence-shattering, I can't imagine what is.

The following Saturday saw Clarets lose 3-1 to a very moderate Cambridge side. The performance was far worse than the result. Even the Clarets' goal was a dodgy penalty. Perhaps most disappointing was the form of Rodaway and James, the two senior players brought in to bolster the Clarets at the start of the season. Rodaway would have been well advised to start his non-League career a season earlier and some of Taffy's play was very indifferent on the day, but with the feeble Rob Regis up front against the gargantuan Lindsay Smith, this was never going to be a contest. It looked fairly apparent that the team was in a dire state.

The Clarets seemed in no immediate danger of relegation, but the thought that if an improvement was not forthcoming soon Burnley could well sink into the danger zone was beginning to cross people's minds. At the end of November, Miller took some positive action and brought in a new signing, centre forward Phil Murphy, and fielded YTS youngsters Peter Leebrook at full-back and Jason Harris up front. This had an immediately positive effect, the Clarets beating Lincoln 3-1 at the Turf and Blackpool 3-2 at Bloomfield Road in the Freight Rover Trophy. The significance of the Lincoln result would not be fully appreciated until the last day of the season. At the time, Lincoln were among the play-off contenders.

The upswing in fortunes did not last, as the side lacked any sort of consistency, except when producing strings of poor results. Another defeat at Southend was followed by a 2-0 reverse at Orient. New signing Murphy had a disappointing match and was completely ineffectual, lacking even the basic ball control required for this level of football, but ineptitude was rife throughout the team and they had the look of a side that couldn't beat an egg.

By this stage the Clarets were in nineteenth position, a whole twelve points ahead of Stockport, who had only 10 points and looked doomed. Rochdale and Torquay were also six and seven points adrift of the Clarets, while Lincoln had 30 points and were in seventh position.

So far, at least the home form had held up, but in December mid-table Cardiff clattered the Clarets in front of another low crowd of 1,702. However, the side had the fortunate knack of pulling off results against some of the better sides, and forced a 2-2 draw at promotion-chasing Wrexham on Boxing Day and, in the following game, they belted Crewe 4-0. After this result there looked to be no danger of the drop. The feeling of comfort lasted only four days. Burnley went into the New Year with 26 points from 22 games, but disaster struck almost before the strains of Auld Lang Syne had faded away.

New Year's Day had Rochdale coming to the Turf. With no disrespect to them, this was one of the more embarrassing fixtures for us. For years, Rochdale people had flocked over to Burnley on a regular basis as Clarets fans. We had played our football three divisions higher. We were the big club and they were the small club on our doorstep. They shouldn't even be coming here for a League game. They did though and went away with all three points, beating us 3-0, a scoreline which flattered us more than them. This was the worst performance of the season – an awful way to start 1987.

Brian Miller and the world's press! (Photo: Burnley Express.)

An even more depressing result was to quickly follow, however, with a 6-0 crushing by Hereford in front of 1,955 spectators. At the time, United were just above the Clarets in the table. Tony Woodworth was making his debut in goal. Everyone was recalling the last time we had given a young goalkeeper a debut, Billy O'Rourke at QPR just over seven years earlier. We were beaten that day 7-0. At least that wasn't going to happen, although by half time it was clear that we were going to be beaten. We were 2-0 down and Woodworth had given away a needless penalty. Hereford added four more in the second half and the scoreline of Burnley 0 Hereford United 6 was the top football headline that night. We had dropped into the bottom four of the fourth division.

Again, remarkably, Miller managed to pull the side around to take a point at fellow relegation strugglers Hartlepool, which might have been three had the Clarets not given two goals away after being two up. Surprisingly, despite the previous week's result, Miller fielded exactly the same line-up except for putting Neenan back between the posts – but then he had no-one else to bring in.

On 4 March, I went, on an inky black night, to watch the Clarets take on Peterborough at London Road. The Posh were looking to get into the promotion hunt on the back of four straight wins, with the Clarets yet to win in 1987. One sensed that a slaughter might well be on the cards. This was one of those games that has been indelibly etched into my brain, for I have never seen a side so outplayed as the Clarets were that night, yet come out with a point.

When considering how close the club came to losing its status, we should thank the Peterborough number 10, who missed four or five chances that night from barn door latch range. Combined with brilliant goalkeeping from Neenan, the score at half time was only 1-0 to the home team. In the second half the Posh were awarded a penalty and, thankfully, the number 10 stepped up to blaze it over the bar. Perhaps realising that the opposition were not going to score again in a month of Sundays, the Clarets rallied and mounted some attacks, which took the Peterborough lads a bit by surprise. Astonishingly, the Clarets managed to equalise, and if you don't believe in miracles and weren't there, I will describe the goal to you. Hampton, with his head down, hoofed the ball aimlessly from the left side of the field to the far side of the Peterborough box to find Grewcock coming in on the blind side of the defence. Neil controlled the ball and fired across goal. The ball was going wide of the far post when a Posh defender diverted it past his own 'keeper. Although Grewcock claimed that goal, I was sat exactly in line with its flight and it was going a yard wide before inept intervention steered it home.

Burnley even had another chance, but somehow loanee Mark Caughey managed to scoop the ball, from one yard out, onto the top of the bar. To give you some idea how bad Burnley were, Hampton got the ball once in the 'Boro half fifteen yards clear of nearest defender, who caught him up in the next fifteen.

After another draw at home to Exeter, the Clarets actually managed to beat somebody, Stockport away, and then they continued the habit of performing well against the better sides, by beating the leaders Northampton 2-1 at the Turf, lifting the side to nineteenth. Once again, however, consistency proved elusive. A string of four defeats followed, coinciding with the absence of the Clarets' most consistent performer, Neil Grewcock. The Clarets were back in deep trouble. Support was falling away again with only 1,846 showing up for the home defeat at the beginning of April against Cambridge.

The transfer deadline passed with no new signings possible. Miller said, 'the club has limited resources, a small squad of experienced players and little scope to strengthen it', and this was the good news! So much for 'the bank that likes to say 'yes', as Brian's attempt to bring in a loan signing floundered on the financial details.

By Easter supporters were beginning to rally round a bit more, perhaps anticipating that these could be the last League games they could ever see Burnley play. A win at Rochdale and a draw with Wrexham on Easter Monday offered some respite for the 4,000 or so who came. However, defeats at Cardiff and Scunthorpe piled on the agony and on 29 April

Rochdale's win over Swansea put the Clarets in bottom place – bottom place of their division and bottom place in the League. After so many years of being the best in the country, Burnley were now ninety-second out of ninety-two, and the situation looked precarious to say the least.

May Day Bank Holiday saw Burnley travel to Crewe for their penultimate fixture. For some reason it was played with a 19.30 kick off, even though all the other games had gone ahead in the afternoon. One by one the results came in and one by one they went against us. By the time the coaches pulled away from Brunshaw Road for Crewe, we knew that nothing other than a win was of any real use. There were 4,175 people packed into Gresty Road, mainly Burnley fans, but it was the home side who struck early through leading scorer David Platt. The score stayed that way until about four minutes from the end when the referee blew his whistle. Free kick? Corner? No, the referee had decided enough was enough and he had blown his final whistle. To be fair we probably wouldn't have scored if we had played until midnight, but then again, as Brian Clough always said, 'It only takes a second to score a goal, young man.' The team came off the field still bottom of the League. A win on the final Saturday against Orient would not guarantee anything. The journey home from Crewe was a long one. There was talk of the game, but most people either sat in silence or recalled the good times. That premature final whistle heralded some of the darkest and worst days ever for Burnley fans.

The next few days were torturous. Our club were headline news on TV, radio and in the newspapers. The other clubs involved weren't getting quite as much media attention, but then they weren't founder members. The club had appealed against the early finish at Crewe but the two linesmen agreed with the referee and that was that. Ex-players were appearing on television, hoping for a miracle. It wasn't a time to be blaming anyone, it was a time to try and rally round. Andy Lochhead, Brian Flynn and an almost tearful Willie Irvine lead the pleas for a result.

By the time Saturday 9 May 1987 came, one of three was going to go down. Ourselves, Torquay United (at home to Crewe) and Lincoln City (away to Swansea). To stay up we had to win and then hope that Torquay didn't and/or that Lincoln lost.

Bottom of Fourth Division with one match to go:

	P	W	D	L	F	A	Pts
Lincoln City	45	12	12	21	45	63	48
Torquay United	45	10	17	18	54	70	47
Burnley	**45**	**11**	**13**	**21**	**51**	**73**	**46**

Turf Moor was a hive of activity from early morning as the vultures arrived. BBC and ITV were there, along with BBC Radio, who were set to cover a Fourth Division match on the World Service for the first time ever. The lunch time programmes featured manager Brian Miller, who claimed to be calm but it didn't take a genius to work out that he was feeling it as much as anyone else. Apart from being the boss he was a fan, a local man. The TV used other angles and the BBC interviewed the then catering manager, Mrs Hilda Denwood, who, like most, struggled to raise a smile. Supporters were arriving from all over the world – not to issue the last rights as some thought, but to offer their help and support. Suddenly people who had long since stopped going to games became aware of what Burnley Football Club meant to them and made their way to the ground, possibly for the last time.

Kick off time arrived with people still trying to get into Turf Moor. The police and referee George Courtney agreed to delay the start by fifteen minutes. With everyone in – 15,781 officially, but believed to be many more – the game finally got under way. It wasn't a classic by any means. Peter Leebrook had to clear from the line very early but just before half time Turf Moor erupted like it hadn't done for many a year as Neil Grewcock gave us the lead. Almost immediately after the restart it was 2-0, Ian Britton scoring with a header at the Bee Hole End. The news coming in from elsewhere was positive, both Torqay and Lincoln were losing, but before we could celebrate Orient pulled one back through Alan Comfort. It didn't matter what happened elsewhere if we didn't win and now we led by just the one goal. Not many inside Turf Moor that day can really tell you how the game went from that point. The Longside just about lifted at around 16:45 as news came in that Lincoln had lost. It was now back in our hands, if we could

Ian Britton scores the second against Orient. (Photo: Burnley Express.)

Tensions relieved as Grewcock puts the Clarets ahead. (Photo: Burnley Express.)

hang on to the lead we were safe. After what felt like an age, Mr Courtney's watch showed 90 minutes and the final whistle of the season blew.

Suddenly the pitch was completely hidden as it seemed the whole town had taken residence on the sacred turf. The relief, elation and sheer joy was so tangible it could have been bottled. A young lad, no more than nine if that, stood clutching his dad's coat with a smile on his face that could have launched a thousand toothpaste ads – it was that kind of feeling.

I recently heard Leighton James describe the game on radio. With two minutes to go, he approached the referee and asked him how long was left. The conversation went something like this:
— 'How long to go George?'
— 'Three minutes.'
James, pointing to the 8,000 people on the Longside terrace went on:
— 'See those people up there?'
— 'Yes.'
— 'Well, they are coming onto this pitch, whether we win or lose, and at the moment, they're coming on happy.'
By James' reckoning, George Courtney proceeded to play out the fastest three minutes of his entire career!

When you look back from the heady heights of Burnley FC today, it's almost inconceivable the state the once-proud club had plummeted to. It's debatable whether they could have even survived the drop: financially they were a wreck; in football terms they displayed no signs that they could have been a force in the Conference; and inevitably crowds would have dropped back below the 2,000 mark or even lower – how long could they have continued in such a manner?

Should promotion come this season, next season, or in five years' time there will be many a Claret sitting in the away end at Old Trafford, Anfield or Highbury who cast a passing thought on events of 9 May 1987. If we ever win the League again, or the European Cup (while we're dreaming, we may as well think big!), it's hard to imagine that the emotion, or the significance, of that day could be surpassed. Burnley were founder members of the Football League. Had it not been for the victory over Orient, one founding member could have been lost forever. The League is a richer place for that win without a doubt.

The celebrations begin. (Photo: Burnley Express.)

Thankful fans carry Ian Britton from the pitch. (Photo: Burnley Express.)

It's heaven for the Claret and Blues. (Photo: Burnley Express.)

Born Again (Newport County)

Neil Williams and George Rowland

1987/88 - Bottom of Division Four and relegated to the Conference
February 1989 - Went out of business
April 1989 - Newport AFC formed
2000/01 - Tenth in Dr Martens Premier League

On Monday 27 February 1989 Newport County died. The courts had finally tired of the endless unmet promises that debts would be repaid; liquidators were appointed, and the club was given forty-eight hours to find £126,000 to pay the preferential creditors. The money was never paid. Over the next week and a half the entire staff were made redundant, the club's assets (down to the last teacup) were systematically cleared and Newport County were officially wound up. Somerton Park was re-possessed by the council, the symbolic padlocking of the gates being witnessed by just two County followers who had turned up to offer a semblance of protest. Everything the club owned was put up for auction three weeks later, perhaps a little too fittingly, on April Fools' Day – it fetched a meagre £12,000. Amongst the lots were twenty-four pairs of amber and black socks, fourteen rolls of tickets, six corner flags, and a numbered goalkeeper's shirt. Nearly eighty years of football in Newport was reduced to 574 lots in a football jumble sale, sold off for the sum of less than a week's wages for some of today's top stars.

Yet, six months later, the amber and black of Newport took to the field again. County may have died, but from the ashes of the old club a new Newport had risen. This was a club founded through the hard work, determination and spirit of County supporters. A club run by the supporters and that was, at last, answerable to the supporters ... goodbye Newport County, hello Newport County AFC.

Newport County had always been dogged with insecurities and problems. Having just reached the giddy heights of the old Second Division in the late 1930s, the outbreak of the Second World War halted the newly-promoted team's hopes of any further progression. When football resumed it was very much a downhill progression. The pre-war impetus was lost and Newport were relegated in the first season after the hostilities ceased, their brief foray into the Second Division having lasted a mere season and three games. Four years after the inception of the Fourth Division in 1958, Newport joined the ranks of those in the League's basement and would not emerge for almost twenty years. Between 1969

Newport County's auction catalogue.

NEWPORT
COUNTY

AUCTION SALE

of the assets of

Newport County Association Football Club Limited
In Compulsory Liquidation

on instructions from the

Joint Liquidators - R.G. Ellis & S.R. Lindsay

SATURDAY, 1st APRIL, 1989.

Viewing - 9 a.m. Auction 10.30 a.m.

CASH ONLY

CATALOGUE
5 0 p

Abbey Auctions Limited
The Maltings, East Dock Road, Newport, Gwent.
(0633) 244459

and 1976, they faced the ignominy of having to apply for re-election to the League on four occasions, including three years in succession. Although never finishing less than third from bottom, it was four times too many for the long-suffering faithful.

The late 1970s saw a significant turn-around in fortunes under the stewardship of first Colin Addison and later Len Ashurst. A sense of belief not seen since the 1930s ran through the club, and from re-election candidates in 1976, Newport progressed to promotion to the Third Division in 1979/80. Entry into the European Cup Winners Cup followed, by way of the club's first and only Welsh Cup triumph. Even this was done the hard way, as the final was against Shrewsbury Town, a team playing two divisions higher in the Football League. Overall, things had never looked better. Attendances rose, as the ground received its first bit of attention in many a year and players actually wanted to come to the club to be part of a future that was looking ever brighter.

The European dream faltered at the quarter-final stage with a creditable 3-2 aggregate defeat at the hands of Carl Zeiss Jena. To say that we were unfortunate not to have made it to the semi-finals would be a massive understatement, with Jena grabbing a last-minute equaliser in the first leg, and then being totally outplayed in the second, only to score with their one attempt on goal. Still, to see the name of Newport County in the hat for a European quarter-final was a moment of unsurpassed pride and joy for all County followers – comparable with, say, Northampton Town making it to the same stage of this year's UEFA competition. It beggars belief, but it happened, albeit with the County faithful pinching themselves more than once to make sure that they weren't dreaming. It looked for so long as if the European triumph would be rapidly followed by a glorious promotion to the Second Division, but, having spent the majority of the 1982/83 season in the promotion zone, a succession of poor results at the wrong time cost County a chance to play with the big boys.

We didn't know it at the time, but that was to be as good as it got for Newport County. Despite the success of the past few years, the club was facing mounting debts, and the battle to stay in business meant that repeated rounds of asset-stripping were necessary. First to be sacrificed were two of Newport's greatest players, John Aldridge and Tommy Tynan. To put the value of these two players into perspective it has to be noted that Aldridge and Tynan were the best double-scoring act in any British League; even Rush and Dalglish at Liverpool couldn't better these two in terms of strike rate, and ironically, although the Liverpool players weren't actually Scousers, Aldridge and Tynan were. Had we been able to hold onto these two, who knows how we could have fared in the years to come?

First to go was Aldridge, sold to Oxford for the paltry sum (even in those days) of £70,000. The club tried to insist that a sell-on clause was included

Somerston Park, home of Newport County.

A despondent scene at Somerston Park.

in the deal, but Oxford were having none of it. Given the fact that Aldridge was out of contract at the end of the season and we might get even less for him if it were to go to a tribunal, Newport reluctantly took the offer on the table. Two years later he was sold on to Liverpool for £750,000. Had the sell-on clause been agreed, it could have been the very thing to have saved Newport.

Tynan left just nine months later, sold to Plymouth for £55,000. Two of the greatest players in Newport's recent past had gone for a combined total of only £125,000. Their replacements were less than adequate and the big slide began, relegation to Division Four in 1987 seeming almost inevitable.

Off the field, the club were facing ever-increasing financial problems. Even after the sale of Somerton Park to the local council, the club's debts amounted to almost £500,000. Desperate fans went to extraordinary lengths to try and stave off the vultures: parachute jumps, auctions, sponsored walks, all sorts of endeavours were made, raising £100,000; but it wasn't enough. The final League season quickly descended into chaos both on and off the pitch.

After a goal-less draw on the opening day, four consecutive League defeats saw County rooted to the foot of the table. It was a position they would occupy for the entire season. Even the seemingly perpetual strugglers of Torquay, Exeter and Rochdale were soon disappearing over the horizon. By the turn of the year, just 11 points had been amassed with a mere 2 wins to show from 24 games. But with the dawning of the New

Players take to the pitch for the final League game against Rochdale.

Year came promises anew. Local businessman Brian Stent took over the chairmanship of the club, declaring that he would bring it back from the brink and ensure a brighter future for County. For the first time in over two years new players were bought – signings with a cash value, as opposed to the long string of free transfers and loanees. Future Welsh international Paul Bodin arrived from Bath for £15,000, along with Dave Brook for a further £6,000. Granted it was relatively small change compared to the seven figure sums exchanging hands in the higher divisions, but for Newport just the ability to part with cash for players was a symbolic triumph. Results picked up briefly – not meteorically – but sufficiently to see Newport double their tally of victories (and almost their points total). However, the wheels of the new board were rapidly coming loose and by February yet another crisis materialised.

Just a month after taking the helm, Stent resigned, claiming that he had not known the true state of Newport's financial plight. He was joined by four more of the fledgling regime, leaving the club with only two directors, brothers Tony and Alan Worthy. The Worthys quickly set about cutting costs. In March the team manager was instructed to sell as many players as possible to raise cash and, to cap it all off, the manager himself was told to leave the club. Not surprisingly, the revival evaporated and Newport remained rooted to the foot of the table.

County had been relegated long before the end of the season, but ironically ended a relegation-material string of results with a 2-0 win at one of the longest journeys of the season away at Darlington. Three hundred travelling supporters celebrated with a conga around Feethams – a rare moment of joy. It was the one solitary win in Newport's final seventeen League games: a run which included three consecutive 4-0 defeats and in which six goals were conceded twice. It was a dire end to a bitter season. The last home game at Somerton Park saw Rochdale take the points in front of 2,560 die-hards. And that was it: it was all over.

The faithful remained optimistic in that close season as hats and T-shirts were produced adorned with 'Newport County Conference Champions 88/89.' The reality was that the finances were so dire that it couldn't be assured that we would even start the first game of the Conference season away at Stafford Rangers. Even the new manager, Eddie May, jumped ship before the season started and it was left to ex-Welsh international John Mahoney to gather

Sixty-eight years of League football come to an end.

39

together enough players to try and start what would be the final season for the Ironsides. A further blow came in early August as the Council, owed a sum of £23,000 in unpaid rent, sought a court order and repossessed Somerton Park. With only twenty-four hours left until the season started, the outstanding amount was finally paid and the keys were handed back. Mahoney, meanwhile, had somehow managed to cobble together eleven players, and the opening match at Stafford Rangers duly went ahead.

If 1987/88 had been a disaster, the following season was soon to descend into a tragic farce. In six months thirty-five players, most of them locals, were brought in as the club struggled just to put out a team. Six of the first seven games ended in defeat, including a record 7-1 home trouncing by Barnet. Just 943 turned up to see the first victory of the season over Maidstone; five years previously, ten times that number had graced Somerton Park.

Amidst the gloom and despondency came the return of Newport's would-be 'knight in shining armour', one Jerry Sherman. Sherman, an American from the town of Newport, Washington, had wanted to take over Newport County for a number of years, purely because he came from a town in America that shared the same name. In what was a complete dream

world he even tried to persuade the faithful that 'when' he took over, he would build a super stadium, which would rival anything else in the country. Rumour had it that the 'Jerrydome' (as fans sceptically referred to it) would even have a retractable roof – ironic really, given that ten years later one of these would be built fifteen miles down the road in Cardiff. On 12 November, Sherman finally achieved his ambition and was named as Newport's new chairman, declaring he would see the club's future secured until 2025 and beyond. By 2000, Newport were to be a First Division club and he would have repaid the faith trusted in him. The truth was that few trusted him, and faith was not the only thing he would not repay. His repeated assurances that he

Newport County's would-be saviour, Jerry Sherman.

Newport County's farewell match, versus Kidderminster Harriers.

would clear all the debts as soon as he 'found out what they all were' only pacified an increasingly dubious High Court for a short time. In the end they heard the same excuse one too many times and, with creditors still unpaid, mainly the Inland Revenue, the Court ordered the club to be wound up.

County's last ever game, a less-than-prestigious Clubcall Cup tie against Kidderminster, summed up a season where the smallest triumphs had been immediately met with ever greater blows. Newport put five goals past the opposition; they scored six in return. The team that took to the field included only one player who had started the campaign, such had been the turnaround of personnel at the club. The programme notes said nothing of the impending court hearing that would serve the final winding up order. As the team left the pitch, a chapter in the footballing heritage of Newport came to a close, albeit unbeknown to the watching fans.

With the club officially closed down six days later, the final kick in the back came with the Conference instructing Enfield to turn up at Somerton Park for a game that quite obviously wasn't going to happen. This gave the Conference the necessary ammunition needed to suspend the club for failing to fulfil its fixtures and in effect we were expelled. Perhaps the only saving grace was that the season's dismal record as the Conference's bottom club would be expunged from the record books.

Final Conference table before Newport County's record was expunged:

	P	W	D	L	F	A	Pts.
Macclesfield	30	6	6	8	56	40	54
Kidderminster H	31	16	6	9	51	40	54
Barnet	30	16	6	8	57	48	54
Wycombe Wanderers	30	15	8	7	61	41	53
Maidstone United	28	15	7	6	64	40	52
Kettering Town	26	15	5	6	39	29	50
Welling United	28	13	8	7	38	27	47
Boston United	28	13	7	8	44	43	46
Runcorn	30	13	6	11	60	44	45
Northwich Victoria	27	11	7	9	46	42	40
Fisher Athletic	29	11	6	12	49	49	39
Telford United	28	10	6	12	33	32	36
Cheltenham Town	28	9	9	10	40	42	36
Altrincham	26	10	6	10	35	37	36
Yeovil Town	29	9	8	12	50	56	35
Chorley	30	10	5	15	40	49	35
Sutton United	25	8	10	7	39	31	34
Enfield	29	9	5	15	43	50	32
Stafford Rangers	29	7	4	18	36	57	25
Weymouth	27	6	6	15	30	53	24
Aylesbury United	29	5	6	18	33	63	21
Newport County	**29**	**4**	**7**	**18**	**31**	**62**	**19**

In the aftermath of the club being made defunct, a group of dedicated supporters, who over the years had striven to raise funds for County, got together to find a way of continuing a football club in Newport at the highest level possible. On 14 April 1989, one day before the Hillsborough disaster, the Lifeline Society met and decided to form a new football club; thus Newport AFC was conceived. A league was found in the pyramid set-up of non-League football that would admit us. The Federated Homes (Hellenic) League was to be our challenge for the forthcoming season, and although it was, in effect, 'Division Seven' in the grand scheme of things, it was a starting point from which to try to regain League status.

That was the easy bit, as the real problems were just about to start again. First, the Borough Council, whilst welcoming the formation of Newport AFC, declined the use of Somerton Park. As an alternative they suggested the use of the 'Glebelands', a park that would just about meet Sunday league football standards. Then the Football Association of Wales refused AFC permission to join the Federated Homes League. To cap it all, the day following the FAW's decision, the Borough Council withdrew permission to use the alternative venue that only three weeks previously they had said we could use.

Within the space of two days, the newly formed Newport AFC had been disowned by their national Football Association and disowned by their local Council. They found themselves homeless with less than two months before their first fixture, and all without the newly formed club having kicked a ball in anger.

Despondency was soon replaced by a resolve to find an alternative home for the new club, in the knowledge that if they failed to start the upcoming season Newport AFC might never even start a campaign. Every club in the neighbouring county of Gloucestershire was contacted with a view to some ground-sharing arrangement being made and to the rescue came Moreton Town. The offer was readily accepted and Newport began their first period in exile. 'Home' games would now consist of an 85-mile trip to Moreton – further away from Newport than some of their 'away' games. But the important thing was that a venue had been found and Newport could begin their battle back to the League in earnest. On 8 June the Hellenic league confirmed Newport AFC's place for the coming season, voting by an overwhelming majority in favour of their admission. Two days later, John Relish, a much admired stalwart and ex-County player, was unveiled as Newport's new manager, and pre-season preparations began.

In the meantime, Jerry Sherman continued to voice his intentions of pursuing his Newport County dream. He threatened all sorts of things over the subject of football in Newport and went as far as to boast that he would resurrect Newport County and have it in direct competition with Newport AFC. Sherman's 'Newport County' even appeared on the Isthmian League's Division Two (South) fixture list for the forthcoming season with an opening game that would clearly never take place scheduled against Horsham. Under the leadership of David Hando, Newport AFC bought the name 'Newport County' for £8,000 in order that it could not be used again, and particularly against the now established new club. With the name as well as the club now out of reach, Sherman was forced to admit defeat and returned to the American Newport.

On 19 August 1989, Newport AFC played their first league game in the Hellenic League, recording a 1-0 victory over Pegasus Juniors. 594 people witnessed the birth of the new club, a substantial number making the 170-mile round trip from Newport for their first 'home' game. In our first season we managed to gain promotion to the Southern League Midland Division. This was something for the Borough Council to be proud of and even the FAW were impressed, so we were granted permission to 'return home.' The Council, quick to jump on the popularity bandwagon, had instigated plans for a new stadium to be built and had even decided to build it to Conference standards. But in the meantime we could use Somerton Park, even though it had been vandalised and looted of anything of use. A merry band of supporters set to work that close season in their own time, using their own tools, and, in a lot of cases, spending their own money on paint and materials to get the ground up to some sort of standard. Newport AFC were able to use this facility for two years before the FAW stepped in again.

The Welsh FA had decided to try and get its house in order and, amidst a barrage of rhetoric about the nation's 'footballing identity', they declared the formation of a Welsh League. At first, we were assured that, although we would be invited to join this new league, there would be no obligation for us to do so. Within a month a total U-turn had been made and they insisted that as we were a Welsh team we must join their set-up. Protestations were made that we should be allowed to continue in the English pyramid, as a means to regaining our League status, but the FAW were adamant that we could not be made an exception. The dual standards in action were clear to all, with Cardiff, Swansea and Wrexham permitted to continue in the English League. Even Merthyr Tydfil were excused, apparently for the solitary reason that they were a Conference side and therefore just one division below the 'hallowed' English League. However, Newport's pleas fell on deaf ears. An appeal was lodged but failed (hardly surprising given the fact that the tribunal to which appeals had to be made consisted of members named by the FAW!). As a Welsh club, Newport were obliged to join the League of Wales – it was as simple as that. If we wished to carry on playing in the English system then we would have to play outside Wales.

So exile it was again, only this time with Gloucester City playing hosts. Exile at Moreton had been accepted reluctantly as a necessary

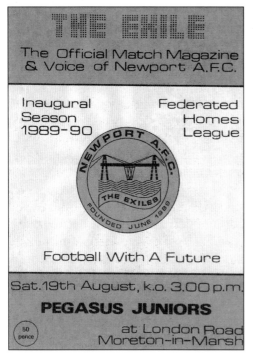

THE EXILE

The Official Match Magazine & Voice of Newport A.F.C.

Inaugural Season 1989-90

Federated Homes League

NEWPORT A.F.C.

THE EXILES
FOUNDED JUNE 1989

Football With A Future

Sat.19th August, k.o. 3.00 p.m.

PEGASUS JUNIORS

50 pence

at London Road Moreton-in-Marsh

evil. A second period of indefinite banishment was a bodyblow that no-one felt inclined to accept. The costs involved in having to play at Gloucester were crippling, not to mention the hardship on the long-suffering fans. Offers of arbitration with the FAW to resolve the impasse were rejected, leaving no other option than to resort to the legal system. Together with Colwyn Bay and Caernafon Town, who were also affected by the edict, a joint fund-raising venture went into operation, with a view to taking the FAW to court for restraint of trade.

It was two years before the legal battle was resolved in Newport's favour. In the meantime an interlocutory injunction had been granted in July of 1994, which provided for us to play our home games in Wales at least until the final ruling. Two further years of exile were thus ended, but the for the real victory we had to wait until April 1995. Justice Blackburne finally judged that we had been treated unfairly and that the FAW's actions constituted an unlawful restraint of trade. At last the FAW were obliged to allow us to return home on a permanent basis and to play our football at the new stadium in Newport. While all this had been going on, the team had responded by winning the championship of the Beazer Homes Midland Division. May 1995 therefore saw a double celebration for all involved with the club.

Now, some five years later, Newport AFC have become Newport County AFC. We remain in the Premier Division of the Dr Martens League, the boot company having taken over from Beazer as the sponsors. The road to the League still remains a long one, but one on which all Newport fans feel grateful to travel. It could so easily have been the case that the club we love had travelled its last journey – the trip into the Conference and then out of business altogether. People like to make comparisons with Aldershot Town who, having gone bust years after Newport County, have managed to reach an equivalent stage in the non-League ladder. But have Aldershot had to go into exile twice for a total of three years? Have they had to take on the power of a Football Association in the High Courts? All of these have cost the club hundreds of thousands of pounds, money which, had it been fed solely into the football club, would have made a big difference to where Newport County AFC are today.

Newport County AFC have proven that there can be life after death, at least in footballing terms. Ten years after the demise of Newport County Mark One, Newport County Mark Two looks forward with optimism, ever striving for the day when we can pronounce ourselves once more a Football League club.

The Ultimate Three Card Trick
(Darlington)

Doug Embleton

1988/89 Bottom of Division Four and relegated to Conference
1989/90 Conference Champions and promoted back to Division Four
2000/01 Twentieth in Division Three

In many ways, Darlo's fall to the Conference was a long time coming. Feethams, the beautiful home of Darlington FC, enjoys a picturesque setting which involves an approach to the 'twin towers' of the main gate (built in 1913 and so pre-dating those pretenders at Wembley!) and a leisurely stroll around the cricket pitch. The ground is ideally situated in the centre of the town, close to the mainline railway station and bus station, not to mention numerous welcoming hostelries.

The football club had always had its intermittent glories. Those worth mentioning include the team of 1957/58, which reached the fifth round of the FA Cup – drawing 3-3 with Chelsea at Stamford Bridge in the fourth round (after leading 3-0) and beating them 4-1 in the replay in extra time – before losing 1-6 to the then mighty Wolves at Molineux in front of 56,000; the team of 1960/61, which ran out of steam for promotion but not before beating Crystal Palace 2-0 and West Ham 3-2 in the inaugural year of the League Cup, eventually losing 1-2 to Nat Lofthouse's Bolton in front of a record 21,000 home crowd; the team of 1965/66, which was promoted from the Fourth Division on one of those (rare) occasions when the board 'speculated to accumulate' – only to return to true form by failing to hold onto one of the best managers the club had ever had in the close season; the team of 1984/85, under the guidance of the dearly departed Cyril Knowles, which also won promotion.

The decline was not a unique phenomenon. Darlington was one of many clubs forever seemingly condemned to rare surges to the second-lowest division interspersed with periods of mid-table mediocrity and the odd skirmish with re-election (in Darlo's case five applications in eleven seasons), dealing with the bank, low attendances, the VAT man (latterly) and the sort of complacency and ordinariness which in so many ways was loveable. Whilst the bigger clubs had their triumphs and huge attendances, there was always something friendly and homely about the trek around the cricket pitch, one of the best steak and kidney pies available and the return journey to the cricket club to warm up with a few beers, the television results and some football banter. The players of both teams would also walk around to the club for a post-match pint and the feeling of community was there for all to see.

Maybe it all became too complacent? Maybe the frequent courting of the danger of 'relegation via non re-election' in the days before the drop to the Conference became a harsh reality was a portent of things to come? Maybe we, the supporters, and the club itself felt we had some God-given right to do this forever? All of this may be true, but when the cold light of relegation reality finally hit home, it was the bitterest of pills to swallow. For those who follow the team regularly, 'Darlo' is the sort of club you love. And, as we all know, we never think of the day when we might lose the one we love.

By the time Brian Little was appointed as Darlington manager in February 1989, the team was in terminal decline. Little did what he could by bringing in his Villa and Midlands contacts (John Gidman and Paul Dyson) and a player from his former club, Middlesbrough (Archie Stephens), but it was too late – the damage was done and the rot had set in.

By the time Darlo played Colchester at home in the penultimate home game of the season, it had reached the stage of 'win or bust'. The kick-off was delayed as over 7,000 souls (more than four times the average gate) walked around the cricket pitch to see Darlo take the lead but, as inevitably happens on the big occasion, eventually lose ... and badly. It was clear that Colchester had learnt their lesson earlier than the Quakers – sacking their manager in January then bringing in Jock Wallace as manager, Alan Ball as coach and goalkeeper Tom McAllister from West Ham United (although it was not enough to stop them being relegated to the Conference the following season, much to the amusement of many Darlington fans).

A huge following made the pilgrimage to Scunthorpe for the final away game of the season, to witness a 1-5 defeat and tearfully salute its fallen heroes. The Conference was an unknown commodity. True, Lincoln had survived the drop and returned, but there were no guarantees. Was this the end of 'Darlo life' as many people knew it? Would Brian Little be the man? The fact that Darlington were finally relegated didn't really sink in until the last home game of the season when a crowd of just over 3,000 came to administer the last rites. The crowd was hoping to go out with a bang, but it was more of a whimper as Darlo, true to form, lost 2-3 to Carlisle United. The crowd that day was a mixture of old and young fans, the hardcore and the transitory, as well as the usual group of 'rubber-neckers' found wherever there is misery, all there to see the curtain come down on sixty-eight years of League football.

Mission Impossible, then a fledgling hand-cranked fanzine but later to become the voice of the fans for the next decade and a thorn in the side of all those who dared to wrong the club, renamed itself *Mission Terminated*. That summed up the feeling that day. For a while, faint hopes were raised when it was suggested that Maidstone United would not be allowed to come into the League. It appeared that their ground might not be up to

Brian Little consoles fans following the 5-1 defeat at Scunthorpe. (Photo: North of England Newspapers.)

scratch as they were ground sharing at Dartford after selling their own ground and so no longer had anywhere to call home. Darlo duly appealed but the protestations came to nought and we were in the Conference – no argument this time. We'd lost the war over the course of the season so we could not complain when this final rearguard action came to nothing.

There were many questions to be asked but, above all, was a feeling of profound sadness. To me, it was akin to the feelings one was supposed to experience when drowning. Flashes of 1953 and 4-1 versus Chelsea and 3-2 versus West Ham ... promotion seasons ... record gates ... allegedly ordinary games which had been highlighted by a moment of genius (or farce) ... humdrum games which had turned into 6-1 thrillers ... no derby next year against Hartlepool – so what exactly was the Conference?

Whilst many younger Darlo fans may have forgotten, or may not even remember, whatever befalls the club from now on, it is an unalienable truth that if it hadn't made an immediate return to the Football League in the first season in the Conference, it may never again have had the opportunity to do so. A decision was taken to remain a 'full-time professional' outfit for this first season in the Conference. The close season, with the talented Brian Little in charge, saw a massive restructuring of the squad with a spending of money which, whilst even then a pin-prick by 'big club' standards, was a major change for Darlo.

With hindsight, it is abundantly clear that the gamble was taken. In other words, even though it was a question of only the Conference Champions

Match programme for the Darlington v. Carlisle match.

The final match before the drop – Darlington v. Carlisle. (Photo: North of England Newspapers.)

winning promotion, the club had adopted Elvis Presley's 'It's Now or Never' as its strategy. Again with hindsight, it could easily have been a case of 'Heartbreak Hotel', 'Surrender' or, in the chairman's case, 'A Fool Such As I'. Little did we know that Welling in Kent would see the scene of 'Let's Have a Party' some ten months later.

Brian Little kept faith in just a few of the relegation squad. Mark Prudhoe, a goalkeeper who more recently was justifiably voted Darlo's Player of the Decade; Les McJannet, an overlapping right-back who had previously been a winger; Jim Willis, an uncompromising central defender whom Little later took to Leicester City for £200,000; Mark Hine, a diminutive but uncompromising midfielder; Paul Emson, a seasoned left winger, probably in the Alan Hinton mode, but quick and experienced, and Archie Stephens, a tough centre forward who had been signed from Middlesbrough towards the end of the previous season.

Notable additions to the squad were Frank Gray, the former Leeds United and Sunderland left-back; David Corner, previously a Sunderland central defender who had played for them at Wembley but for whom injuries had probably slowed him down to Conference and lower League level (at which, I hasten to add, he was a genuine 'star'); Andy Toman and John Borthwick, midfield and centre forward respectively, both signed from local rivals Hartlepool United for a total of £48,000; David Cork, a skilful striker who had once been an Arsenal apprentice – not a 'breaker down' of defences, more a close control, flick-on type of player – and finally Kevan Smith, a captain, central defender and former Darlo player who had since been with Rotherham, Coventry and York City, for another £10,000.

With a few other 'retained' players, youth players and signings, this was the bulk of the squad that lined up for the Conference campaign. Right from the off, there was an attraction in seeing 'new' teams visiting Feethams. The first game against Kidderminster Harriers attracted a crowd of nearly 3,000 and it was unusual to see the opposition playing in green and white 'quartered' shirts. The 3-0 win was, of course, an added bonus. On the following Bank Holiday Monday (how lucky to have two home games as a starter) we demolished Northwich Victoria 4-0. New – but now familiar chants – emerged from our mini-Kop, the Tin Shed, such as 'Come in a taxi, you must have come in a taxi'.

With the prospect of fewer away fans visiting Feethams, the smallest side of the ground had been allocated to visiting supporters for most games. Since it was one of the last seasons when it was possible to walk around the ground and change ends at half time, Darlo's forwards were vocally encouraged by large behind-the-goal crowds in each half.

The game against Northwich Victoria revealed just how much progress Brian Little and player-coach Frank Gray had made. The team played the ball on the ground, with possession football from the back five all the way to the forward line and in the first dozen or so games the fitness and cohesion achieved by a pre-season of full-time professional fitness and tactics training really showed through. Indeed, the lengthy unbeaten run at the start of the season was the foundation of the ultimate championship success. Such an approach was crucial as pressure was to be on Darlo throughout the campaign with many Conference sides raising their game just that bit more against us – ever keen to put one over on the ex-League team. And a few did just that.

This was also the time when the elder of my two daughters caught the Darlo bug that has now been handed down through four generations of my family ... maybe it was the pies, maybe it was the thighs! Maybe it was David Cork's long, dyed, blond hair or maybe it was 'being with Dad', anyway she caught the bug and went on to enjoy the two most eventful seasons in the club's long history. Living, as I did, some thirty miles away from Darlo and with a hectic job and young family, our Darlo-watching was largely confined to all home games via season tickets and ears glued to the local radio for away games.

The football was a joy to watch. It was also a unique experience to have to qualify for the FA Cup first round, which we did, and then to feature on *Match of the Day* as one of the Conference sides beating a League club (Halifax). It was also nice to feature regularly on local television (the local BBC had lost the rights to show summaries of League games at the time).

In fact, we seemed to be receiving more coverage than in many of our years as a humdrum lower-division League club and maybe this is one of the truisms of the dreaded drop into the Conference. It might have been that the media were merely being vultures waiting to see our failure to return to the League but it still seems to hold true that the fallen do receive immediate media coverage. Some of our games towards the end of the season were featured in the Sunday Press and the coverage on local TV transcended the usual 'blink and you'll miss it' or 'sorry, the cameraman had the DTs'-style and became mini-documentaries of key away games, such as the one at Barnet.

What of Barnet? They emerged as our key rivals and were the first team to beat us, 2-1, at Brian Little's 'Fortress Feethams'. One thing which struck me early on in the season was that the fans and players of the Conference sides of that era were still in the 'beautiful game' mode. Perhaps this was the beginning of the end of this period since automatic relegation/promotion to and from the Conference was a relative novelty.

I remember having to sit in the main box (due to a ticketing cock-up) at an early season home game against Stafford Rangers. This was just at the time when other Conference teams were gaining an 'Autumn fitness' and sense of tactics which were catching up with our own. They gave us a really hard game as we ground out a flattering 2-1 home win. Their squad players who were not on the pitch were sat close to us in the stand and I gained the immediate impression that these were largely guys who could have made a full-time living in at least lower full-time Leagues but who also had better than average jobs and careers (and possibly intelligence) and therefore combined these with a semi-professional role in football.

As the season unfolded, we made a few more imaginative signings. Gary Gill, a £20,000 capture from Middlesbrough, who could fill a range of midfield roles; Phil Linacre, also for £20,000, a striker who never really overcame his proneness to injury; Steve Mardenbrough, a tricky winger who was to become a key player for several seasons; and Gary Coatsworth, a utility player who was to have the final say in our Conference Championship. The club even began making videos of home games and the end of season video product, whilst truly appalling in terms of continuity, lack of commentary and complete lack of the game which clinched the Championship, remains a cherished item.

One memorable midweek game was a 6-1 victory over Boston United. Played on a rainy and windswept Tuesday evening on a gluepot of a pitch, Darlo – and especially David Cork, who grabbed four goals – played out of their skins. However, whilst all of the goals were memorable, my abiding memory is of the dozen or so hardy Boston fans standing on the chilled, wet, open terrace and dancing a conga (heartily applauded by the Darlo fans) when Boston scored their single consolation goal.

Throughout the season Barnet remained our main threat and, looking back, it is very interesting that our two last-minute wins against Welling United provided the really lucky six points which gained us promotion. Although you win a championship over a whole season, you often turn the campaign on one or two games; these are the slices of luck which are so often crucial to success.

David Geddis, another one of Brian Little's signings, was an ex-Ipswich and England under-21 player who had been badly injured earlier in his career in a car crash. He clearly still carried a stiff back (which was probably damned painful, making him all the more a hero) but Little was wise enough to know that when the going got tough in terms of pre-promotion tension, it was always going to be useful to call upon players such as this, even for a thirty minute spell as substitute.

In a rearranged home game with Welling on an early Spring evening and with the clock rapidly ticking towards the whistle and a 0-0 draw, Darlo won one final corner. With this still being the days when the behind-the-goal crowd could change ends at half-time, the Darlo supporters (I swear) half sucked the ball into the net, but it was David Geddis, using all of the know-how of a seasoned professional who had played in the top flight, who cleverly steered the ball towards the goal with his head.

The press always loves a clash of the titans and in the Conference this took the form of Darlo's visit to Underhill at the end of March. The hype was built up in true boxing-match fashion and Barnet recorded a then record crowd of 5,880. The match itself was never one to set pulses racing, but was in the end a contest of men against boys. Brian Little's tactics worked a treat as disciplined performance and a goal in each half saw off Barry Fry's boys. The travelling Quaker fans (whose anthem, 'The Only Way is Up', was sung to the tin rafters) were delirious and were transported by express Northern Line trains into the centre of London – where they continued their celebrations, some unaware of the Poll Tax riots that were still going on around in the streets around them.

Having lost our penultimate away game to Kidderminster 2-3 – and in the last minute, when a 2-2 draw would have done it – further pressure was added. We had started the season with two home games, including a 3-0 win over Kidderminster. We ended the season with two away games and the first of these had been a 2-3 defeat ... to Kidderminster. Revenge must have been sweet for the Harriers. And so it all came down to the final away game at Welling.

Darlo took a huge number of fans to the Park View Road Ground. People travelled from afar – not just from Darlo, as Quakers-in-exile from all over the UK were there for what was in most respects a typical end-of-season game, with bright sunshine, shirtsleeves and a bone hard pitch.

Four things strike me about this game. Firstly, for the second time running, we beat Welling 1-0 with an 'almost last minute' header from a player who was not a regular member of the squad. Gary Coatsworth had been an invaluable utility player who had covered

Approaching the Feethams' 'Twin Towers' before the final home game of the Conference season. (Photo: Doug Embleton.)

53

Darlo fans await news of Barnet. (Photo: North of England Newspapers.)

full-back, central defence and midfield on intermittent occasions. The looping header which won the game was the most extreme I will ever witness. From a free kick on the left, Gary made contact and the ball headed skywards before (oh so slowly) soaring up and over the Welling 'keeper's head, who – no matter how quickly he scrambled back – could not make contact.

The second thing was just how well Brian Little had judged the season and this final game. When, in the second half, it was clear that a draw would suffice, he brought on seasoned campaigners like David Geddis who, even though he was playing in a defensive role and even though his back was so bad it would have taken a McAlpine Crane to turn him, had all of the necessary 'savvy', (both positional and verbal) to stay calm and in control.

The third thing was that I would actually miss the Conference for its good football, its friendly fans and its lack of pretence. Indeed, I even wrote to Welling United and they wrote back by return.

The fourth was just how momentous the season had been. The rumour was that Darlo would have given it only one season as a fully professional outfit and that if promotion had not been achieved they would have been forced to go semi-professional.

The joy and ecstasy at the end of the game will live with me forever. Maybe it was the reverse sensation of 'drowning' when we went down in the previous season. Almost like hitting the bottom and floating back up ... with Gary's header at Welling and then the final whistle being like the moment when, having held your breath, you finally break through the water and hit the air.

The celebrations of Gary's goal even featured in *The Homes of Football*, a wonderful collection of photographs by Stuart Clarke, with the title 'Darlo's Tortured League – Exile Over'. The Darlo T-shirts for that season called it 'The Days of Exile Tour' and I'm sure that whilst this was the brave face of football faith it certainly was a relief when that goal looped in.

The journey home was 'pure belter'. It was my birthday as well. What a day ... what a season. What happened next is another chapter in Darlo folklore.

With only one more astute signing, Mick Tait, on a free transfer, Brian Little retained the system and tactics and took Darlo to a straight second championship by winning the Fourth Division, again on the last day of the season. Unarguably, the team had accustomed itself to 'controlled' away performances (Little's teams do tend to grind out 1-0 away victories) and enough adventure to win home games during the exile in the Conference.

Equally unarguably, the platform for this sustained success was the decision to remain fully professional during the first season in the Conference. Maybe we had to hit the bottom before bouncing back up? Maybe, after a long period of indifference and accepting 'survival', the relegation to the Conference was the kick up the backside which the club needed? Whatever the truth of the matter, many of the supporters who are loyal and true today are people who were attracted to the club in its Conference season.

Some of the highlights were a magnificent 0-0 draw away to local rivals Hartlepool on a rain-swept day and on a pitch which was a mixture of mud and sand. Whilst increasingly outplayed, Darlo withstood the storm and goalkeeper Mark Prudhoe had what was probably his best and bravest game for the club. With only a few games to go, there was a memorable 3-0 win at a sunny and warm Northampton when Darlo went three up within the first 17 minutes and then just closed the game down. This game probably saw our best goal of the season – a sweeping move down the right wing involving Toman and McJannet and then the sweetest of all volleys from Mitch Cook, another of Brian Little's shrewd signings who was in his second spell with the club. The goal was so crisp, clinical and swift that the 1,000 or so Darlo supporters behind the other goal were as stunned as the home supporters and there was a five-second pause before the usual 'away goal' eruption. The goal looked even better the following day on local TV.

Sadly, the club resumed its normal habits once it reached the dizzy heights of the (then) Third Division. With the departure of Brian Little to Leicester – (and he took key defender Jim Willis and Gary 'looping header' Coatsworth with him for a combined fee of £215,000) – and the usual refusal at the next fence of a speculate-to-accumulate policy, Darlo tumbled straight back to the Fourth.

After another six or seven years of false dawns, false prophets (and, at times, false profits!), the club faced extinction but this time not via relegation to the Conference but by the threat of bankruptcy. A by now well-known saviour in the shape of George Reynolds rode into town and promised Premiership football, a new stadium and no repeats of the 'rape and pillage' regimes who had been in control of our beautiful club.

At the time of writing, the jury is still out. After a defeat in our second Wembley play-off of the 1990s, the squad was broken up and crowds have again slumped. The Conference at times seems a million miles – well, at

Darlo skipper Kevan Smith brings back the Fourth Division trophy to the cricket club bar.

least ten years – away, but there is a nagging feeling that history might just repeat itself.

Can we say that anything was learned from those wonderful two seasons with Brian Little? It seems not. In my view there were maybe five key lessons that could have seen the club truly build on the successes of those marvellous years: firstly, crowds will eventually come back to see a winning team. The Conference season saw Darlo double its home gate and built even further on this when we won the Fourth Division Championship. Secondly, success does breed success. The winning habits of the Conference season were carried seamlessly into the Fourth Division and at the minimal extra cost of one single free transfer player. Thirdly, the winning ways in unfamiliar surroundings increased Darlo's travelling away support. Many people came along for the fascination of visiting grounds and towns which (they surely hoped) they would only ever visit once. This tradition of strong away support persists to this day, aided and abetted by the formation of the exile-supporters group, DAFTS (Darlo Away Far Travelling Supporters). Fourthly, speculation after relegation did pay off. The squad which was assembled to bounce back into the League at the first attempt proved good enough to continue the 'bounce' upwards. This is also a reflection of the excellent standard of football in the Conference where the likes of Efan Ekoku (Sutton United) and Stan Collymore (Stafford Rangers) lined up against the Quakers. Finally, the success gave the club back its heart and soul.

To have squandered this and for the Darlo to have come so close to bankruptcy only seven years later, even after continued providing revenue from outgoing players – the sales of Preece (Aberdeen), DeVos (Dundee United), Gregan (Preston), Blake (Bradford), Appleby (Barnsley), Pollitt (Notts County), Coppinger and Robinson (Newcastle) alone amounted to £2.2 million – is nothing short of scandalous. It is also an insult to the feats of the Conference winning side.

If Darlington FC are ever to move away from being a team which will intermittently flirt with the dangers of bankruptcy or relegation to the Conference (and let's face it, if relegation to the Conference had existed from the late 1970s to the mid-1980s, Darlo would have been down well before it actually happened) they may have to re-learn some of the lessons of ten years ago. The Conference season was memorable. It was also enjoyable and it catalysed the rebirth of the club. If it happened again, it is doubtful whether we would make such a comeback.

Last time, the dangers of relegation weren't truly recognised until it was too late. The present chairman's money, and rhetoric, may well allay all of these fears. For a club such as Darlo, one relegation to the Conference can be forgiven. A second time would be an act of gross mismanagement ... even 'Bravehearts' would not withstand the tension of another 87th minute looping header.

Darlo fans invade the pitch at Welling at the final whistle. (Photo: Doug Embleton.)

THE FALL AND RISE OF
COLCHESTER UNITED

Matt Hudson and Kevin Scott

1989/90 Bottom of Fourth Division and relegated to Conference
1991/92 Conference Champions and promoted to Division Three
2000/01 Seventeenth in Division Two

On the final day of the 1997/98 season, Colchester travelled to Doncaster. A win against Rovers, combined with other results going our way, meant we could be promoted automatically. For the fans of Doncaster, it was a day of altogether different emotions. Relegation from the Football League had long since been confirmed, and this would be their last game before dropping into the Conference.

In a scrappy game interrupted by at least two pitch invasions, Colchester won 1-0, but results elsewhere meant that we would have to endure the stress of the play-offs yet again. It all seemed so irrelevant. When the final whistle went at Belle Vue, the Rovers' fans were on the pitch with their heads in their hands, not really wanting to leave the ground. We sat on the pitch talking to their supporters, who were afraid to go home, because that would spell the end of their reign in the bottom rung of the League.

It was something of a surreal scene. Some fans had brought their own ball along, and were playing in the net where Colchester had scored the goal that we had hoped might be enough to send us up. Meanwhile, the players had come out onto the balcony to take the sympathetic applause, but the overwhelming feeling was one of emptiness – whilst a lot of fans remained, many left as soon as the final whistle blew, and Belle Vue became something of an empty shell.

For many of the Doncaster fans we spoke to, the feeling was that the drop out of the League was a point of no return. Most of their season had seen them fielding a side made up of players from the Unibond Premier League coupled with YTS lads. Their record was almost the worst of any club in the League's history. The mismanagement at the club is now legendary, and at this point in time it was a wonder that there was still a club left. They never really had a chance.

And that's why I think we were lucky to drop out of the League when we did. Ten or so years ago, the gap between Division Three (or the Fourth Division as it was then) and the Conference was a massive one. Few, if any, of the Conference sides were full time, so the gap in fitness and professionalism was clear to see when we started our assault on an immediate return to the League. These days though, the top ten or so clubs in the Conference are comparable to most in Division Three, so any side dropping through the trapdoor faces a much more difficult challenge to instantly return. Granted the circumstances at Doncaster were very different to those we faced back in the early 1990s, but you only need look as far as Hereford and Scarborough to see that the days of relegated clubs bouncing straight back have gone. That day at Belle Vue showed us how lucky we really were – we had gone down, but had returned. If it happened today, who knows how long we would spend in the wilderness?

About two weeks after the Doncaster game we were at Wembley, to face Torquay in the Division Three play-off final. A David Gregory penalty meant that we defeated the South Coast side on a wet Friday night. In the space of eight years, we had gone from complete desolation, dropping out of the League, to our highest position for years and promotion to the Second Division. Two other visits to Wembley during that time tells you that the Conference experience wasn't all bad for us!

The U's relegation had been on the cards for a couple of years when it eventually came in 1989. The turning point for the club had been the departure of Mike Walker two years previously. At the time of his exit from Layer Road, Walker had taken the club to the top of the division, via seven consecutive wins. He was awarded the divisional manager of the month and was promptly sacked. Apparently United's chairman, Jonathan Crisp, had fallen out with him – the truth of the story never really came out (not

U's fans after the final League game. (Photo: Colchester Evening News.)

a plausible story anyway) – and that was that. An unknown and inexperienced hard-man, Roger Brown, was brought in, to universal incredulity. Within months the club were tumbling down the division; Mike Walker, meanwhile, went on to take Norwich into the UEFA Cup. A lot (and I mean a lot) of long-term Colchester fans stopped bothering to turn up.

Various big names were subsequently brought in to manage the club: Jock Wallace, Alan Ball and Mick Mills all took a turn, but to no avail. The U's finished second from bottom to Darlington, and then finally bottom. Certainly there was great deal of despair among the fans, coupled with very real anger at the chairman. At the same time though, Lincoln had bounced back from the Conference at the first attempt and there was an undercurrent of expectation that if the team could be held together, we could do the same.

Ian Atkins took the team to a very strong position throughout most of the first year in the Conference, and with only a few games left it was us or Barnet. It eventually went down to the wire but, at the crunch, it was Barnet who took the honours. Atkins departed in the summer, and the club made the appointment which would seal their return to the League fold – former U's stalwart Roy McDonough was named as Atkins' replacement. McDonough had played for Colchester in the 1980s when both they and he were good. He had left on very bad terms, however, after blaming the fans' barracking for the suicide of his fellow striker John Lyons. So it was something of a surprise when he returned from Southend. McDonough's reputation was prodigious. The most sent-off player in League history, always spoiling for a fight, always arguing with referees, but a huge favourite in spite of all that ... or perhaps because of all that.

The story of Colchester in the Conference is the story of Roy McDonough and the team that he led. United, despite their small scale, had always behaved, and always been thought of, as a proper professional club with some degree of pedigree. Big Roy, frankly, changed all that. Colchester under Roy had the air of an astoundingly talented pub team. They played dynamic, fluid, passing football, scored goals almost at will, and yet came across as a bunch of lads out for a laugh and a casual kick-around. To add to the reputation they were building, Roy and various players would regularly hold court in The Lamb in Colchester High Street and, as far as I can gather, were renowned for sinking more than a few pints.

There was a lot of worry that the club would be unable to stay professional for a further year, but the bold decision was made by the new chairman, James Bowdidge, to continue as such. As a result, we remained full-time in a division still largely populated by postmen and factory workers. The season turned out to be without a doubt the most successful and the best humoured at Layer Road in three decades. Colchester were clearly superior to all-comers (a rare, rare thing, believe me), and it was all

Roy McDonough. (Photo: Colchester Evening Gazette.)

done in this fantastic lads-on-the-booze atmosphere. Even Wycombe, who were to tie with us on points, never really seemed a threat. It was like Steve Redgrave et al in the Olympics; it might have looked a close thing, but it never seemed it to us. As it turned out, promotion on the final day of the season was never really in doubt. Barrow were rock bottom of the table and,

61

if we won, Wycombe had to win by five more goals than us. When we went two or three up really early on, an eight-goal win for Wycombe seemed unlikely and the party could really start. Barrow were eventually dispatched by five goals, with American (super) hero Mike Masters grabbing an impressive hat-trick and the crowd lifting the roof off of Layer Road (well, we would have done if we'd had one!). After two years we had done it – we were back in the League.

Two weeks or so later, we had the chance to complete a historic double. Following a club like Colchester, the Twin Towers seemed so far away, an unachievable dream if you like, but here we were, on our way up to London to face Witton Albion in the FA Trophy final. More than 20,000 people made the trek up to Wembley, and we outnumbered the opposition fans by about four to one.

The sending off of Jason Cook took a little of the shine off of the day, but two early goals, as Mike Masters again showed his class, meant that the right result was always within our reach and, thankfully, we didn't throw it away, eventually running out 3-1 winners. I don't know if it was just the feel-good factor of having done a league and cup double, but at this time a real sense of community had returned to the club. For the first time in years being a Colchester supporter was something you were proud to admit to in an area dominated by Arsenal, Liverpool and Ipswich (Manchester United were

Nicky Smith celebrates with the crowd. (Photo: Colchester Evening Gazette.)

Victory against Barrow. (Photo: Colchester Evening Gazette.)

only just starting on their winning ways at this stage, of course) fans. The 'Back to the League' appeal summed this up, and the sight of the fans turning up at Layer Road brandishing their paintbrushes was one to behold – everybody mucked in order to get the ground up to scratch and pass the Football League guidelines.

Having gone up, we were suddenly the small fry in the division once again. Nine years on and we are still the small fish, but now we're in our third year as small fish in the Second Division pond. There has been murmuring amongst the fans that the club is at something of a crossroads. After two seasons in this division, one for adaptation and one for consolidation, many fans would like to see the club start to progress and advance. As it stands, we are in the same position in the division that we have been since arriving in 1998. Success this season (2000/01) would be thirteenth position or somewhere around there.

At least the club learnt their lesson when it came to the sale of Lomana Tresor Lua Lua. We had been short-changed to a ridiculous degree when we sold Mark Kinsella to Charlton for £150,000, but with Lua Lua we held firm for the right amount. To get £2.25 million for a player with very little League experience was no mean feat, and it meant that the club finally had some money in the kitty. There is no doubt that at present the team is still finding its feet in the post-Lomana era, but in time, the money reaped from his transfer will come in very handy for a side that is losing almost £400,000 a season.

It would appear to some that we are being ungrateful for the fact that we are only seventeenth in Division Two, given that only a decade before we were out of the League. Yet, having got this far, there is a feeling that we should not rest on our laurels. With the NTL TV deal about to come into place for the Nationwide sides, the difference between being in this division and Division Three is around £400,000 a season – something that's not to be sniffed at, clearly.

But there seems a real reluctance to grab this opportunity by the throat and really go for it. With no apparent progress on the pitch over the last twenty-four months, the fans are beginning to drift away, and the current average has dropped over the last two seasons. For the wider public in Colchester, survival is not an attractive proposition, the chances are the fans would prefer to be back in 1996 where we were challenging for the play-offs season after season. To use a Premiership analogy, the club has a choice as to be a Leicester or a Derby. Leicester managed to avoid an instant return to Division One after their play-off promotion, and after a couple of seasons of consolidation, they began to use their cash to bring in players and strengthen the squad – with the current success showing that was the way to go. Many other sides, for example Derby or Forest, have failed to make that speculative investment, and are paying the price for it now. The fact is that, even at this level, success has to be an immediate thing to keep everybody happy. As Luton showed recently by their dismissal of Ricky Hill after only five months in charge, fans and boards want success in the short term – even at Division Two level managers do not have the luxury of long term planning.

If they wanted to, Colchester are ideally placed to advance into mid-table security and possibly even a promotion push. Located within an hour of London (when the trains are running properly), the U's should be able to attract the young players forced out of clubs like Tottenham, Arsenal and West Ham due to the influx of foreign players (and with the money from Lua Lua's sale, such players' demands could now be met). But it's going to take a fundamental change in the club's thinking if this is to be achieved. In reality, the 'small club' mentality means that we will probably continue where we are for a few years if we're lucky, and then return to the bottom division, from whence we came. The days when we saw ourselves in the same light as clubs like Sheffield Wednesday and Blackburn are truly gone; these days, it's Scunthorpe and Hartlepool.

For the last decade we have lived and built on two glorious years of rejuvenation in the Conference. Two years of success brought the crowds back to Layer Road, buoyed the club, and gave it the foundations upon which we have developed to the point where we enjoy our (relatively) lofty position today. The club now needs to take the next step, and to begin thinking like a Division Two club with aspirations rather than a club 'on loan' from the basement division. It needs to replicate the bold thinking of the Conference years and translate the ambition of those seasons into Division Two terms.

Much of this will hang on the potential new development at Cuckoo Farm. Since selling the leasehold of Layer Road to the council, the club have been looking all over the local area to find a location for a new ground and a site, just off the A12, has been selected. As of January 2001, the club stands as close as it ever has to gaining full planning permission for a new 10,000 stadium on the outskirts of the town. The belief is that a new stadium will regenerate interest in the club, and attract new supporters that find the current ground less than hospitable. The revival in fortunes of Northampton Town since the move to Sixfields is a case in point. The club has, to date, fulfilled its part of the bargain on the pitch, but as things stand has probably gone as far as it can with current resources. The value of a new ground cannot be underestimated, and it is down to all supporters of our beloved club to lobby the relevant authorities and ensure that the move goes ahead.

Otherwise there is no doubt we will be back in the bottom division, and most probably for an elongated stay. Worse still, God forbid, we could find ourselves once more facing the Conference; but this time not a welcoming part-time, easy-to-get-out-of Conference, but an altogether different proposition from which escape is much less likely. We could find ourselves in the same boat as Doncaster, Hereford and Scarborough, and face the same feelings as the Donny fans on the final day of 1997/98. Relegation for Colchester the first time around was, perversely, a positive thing for the club; were it to come a second time, it could mean the end of Colchester as a League outfit on a permanent basis.

Fans take to the field after the Barrow game. (Photo: Elaine Soame.)

BACK IN THE FOLD (HALIFAX TOWN)

Johnny Meynell

1992/93 Bottom of Division Three and relegated to Conference
1997/98 Conference champions and promoted back to Division Three
2000/01 Twenty-third in Division Three

It was former Halifax Town chairman John Crowther who said that the Football League's introduction of automatic relegation and promotion between the Fourth Division and the Conference in 1986/87 probably prolonged Halifax Town's own Football League status. Regularly found going cap in hand to the Café Royale for the Football League's AGM, Halifax Town had clung onto their Fourth Division status through re-election no less than five times since they were demoted to the bottom division in 1976. Crowther himself had been instrumental in Halifax's re-election in 1981, when he lobbied most of the Football League chairmen to secure their votes. He may have been proved correct with his prediction, for following the abolition of the re-election system, Halifax Town were bottom four material in each of the four seasons before they finally succumbed. The rest of the Football League would have surely lost patience.

The 1992/93 season would prove to be perhaps the darkest in the club's history, yet no one could really say that relegation that year was never on the cards. Halifax Town had been living on borrowed time. And, in fact, they could on numerous occasions have disappeared of their own making, narrowly surviving many a financial crisis, the most recent coming in 1987 under John Madeley of the well-known DIY stores. Yet here they were, still alive and just about kicking, with Jim Brown as chairman, and John McGrath, the former Newcastle United and Southampton stopper, as manager. Where previous incumbents of the Shay hotseat had failed to transform the fortunes of our ailing club, Brown had turned to McGrath after being impressed with the way he had breathed new life into Port Vale and Preston. At Deepdale, he had turned a side that were re-election campaigners in 1986 to one that finished as runners-up to Northampton the very following season. The fans too must have thought that here was the miracle worker that they had prayed for, but sadly, the downward spiral Halifax Town had found themselves on somehow just became faster and faster.

McGrath arrived at the Shay as successor to Jim McCalliog in October 1991, and immediately began to stamp his own personality on the place. Oshor Williams, his erstwhile sidekick, was brought in and new players,

Pre-season photocall for the fateful 1992/93 season. (Photo: Keith Middleton.)

that we hoped would improve things, came in good numbers. There were, however, raised eyebrows when McGrath shelled out a whopping £45,000 for goalkeeper Lee Bracey, who automatically took the number one spot from future Scotland and Celtic 'keeper Jonathan Gould. The addition of left full-back Paul Wilson was deemed a slightly better bargain, costing only £30,000 from Northampton, but what was clear to most Town fans was that we lacked real quality. When McGrath saw fit to sell our star striker Steve Norris in January 1992, we seriously questioned his intentions. Norris, after all, had been our saviour the previous season, the scorer of 30 League goals – more than half Town's total tally – and winner of the Football League's Golden Boot award. All of sudden we had no potent goalscorer, but that season, we didn't really need one, did we? After all, once Aldershot had resigned from the League, Halifax Town knew that they were safe from the dreaded drop for at least one more year.

But, at the start of the 1992/93 season, we expected something more, and rightly or wrongly thought we'd got it when McGrath unveiled the former Liverpool, Brighton and Southampton hard man Jimmy Case. Mick Matthews, who'd been a sort of hit at the Shay a few years earlier, returned to the fold, and on the eve of the opening game at Rochdale, Howard Gayle, who once had run Bayern Munich ragged in a European Cup semi-final for Liverpool, joined the club. Surely we were on to a winner?

Well, we were in that first game. Two spectacular volleys from Ronnie Hildersley, and a Paul Wilson penalty saw us through 3-2 at Spotland, but unfortunately the spirit shown in the sun that fine afternoon was hardly repeated throughout the course of the season. This was particularly the case at home, where the total of Halifax victories amounted to just three paltry victories from twenty-three home matches. The Football League fixtures messed Halifax up in a big way during the first weeks of the season. Once they had entertained Scunthorpe the following Saturday, the fixture list deemed that Town would play their next three games away from home, and by the time they had lost them all, at Cardiff, Crewe and Lincoln, we were bottom of the pile.

Suddenly, McGrath's misfit team of players who had served him a little better in an earlier age, such as so-called strikers John Thomas and Nigel Greenwood, looked as likely to get us out of trouble as a the Keystone cops in a Halifax kit. In an effort to put some life into the forward line, McGrath moved Ian Thompstone out of the heart of defence, and was paid instant dividends when Tommo netted a hat-trick in a sensational 5-2 win at Northampton. At that point, we were happy the club was moving in the right direction, and the defeat of Gillingham on 10 October carried Halifax up to tenth place. We were sitting pretty, weren't we?

The fact was, though, that sensational victories away from home were not mirrored in any shape or form at home. Little did we realise it then, but following that victory over Gillingham Town, we would only win one more game at the Shay before the season's close. Suddenly, defeat followed defeat, and before we knew where we were, we were in a dogfight. Unfortunately for us, we didn't have the players who could pull us out of it.

This became particularly apparent at Marine, whom Town travelled to face in the FA Cup in November. Town's record against non-League opposition was not one to brag about, but though we knew Roly Howard's side were going to give their all in the game, we did at least expect our players to show a bit of heart. What was actually served up by the players was one of the most gutless performances ever by a Halifax side, and Marine's 4-1 victory in no way flattered them. But the Halifax camp weren't all pulling in the same direction. Why else would Alan Kamara and Ronnie Hildersley see fit to sit out the game in the nearest boozer whilst their team-mates brought shame on the club?

That defeat at Marine couldn't have come at a worse time. Just two days later the board of directors met to discuss whether Halifax Town had indeed got a future at all. Not for the first time, the club was highly in debt, and the plug being pulled was a distinct possibility. I was one of a few hardy souls who stood outside in the cold to hear first hand whether we'd have any club to support the following week. Unless you have been in the position, it's impossible to imagine not knowing whether your club will exist come Saturday; whether or not your results will be expunged and your name deleted from the League records – it doesn't bear thinking about. Jim Brown and his cronies elected to review the situation in the New Year, and we had some breathing space.

But it was business as usual on the park, and with Town's position

Mick 'Basil' Rathbone. (Photo: Keith Middleton.)

looking ever more precarious going into December, boss John McGrath literally jumped ship and left it sinking in his absence. The supporters cannot really say we were sorry to see him go, but what we really expected then was for the board to appoint someone who might be able to take our club away from trouble. Some of us expected Jimmy Case, who on the face of it would have seemed a natural successor to McGrath, to get the nod. Even McGrath's assistant, Oshor Williams, was mentioned (thankfully the board didn't consider him). So you can imagine our surprise when Mick Rathbone, our physiotherapist, was appointed.

Basil, as we all affectionately called him, had a good background in the professional game, having made more than 350 League appearances with Birmingham City, Blackburn Rovers and Preston. But his chosen career after injury curtailed his playing days was as a physiotherapist. We really questioned the wisdom of giving Rathbone the job. Not that he wasn't a popular fellow – Basil was one of the nicest guys in football – but when did nice guys ever succeed? Stories later came out that occasionally he didn't know what team to pick and sought advice from the chairman, but that may have been just speculation.

What wasn't speculation was the fact that Town needed a quick fix. Rathbone took Mike Williams on loan from Sheffield Wednesday – he was a hit with the fans and we wanted to keep him until the end of the season at least. Initially, performances improved. Around a thousand of us made the trip to see Town outplay second-placed York City and earn a merited draw, and we could be forgiven for thinking we had turned a corner. Especially when, in our next game away at Darlington, we won 3-0, with another new recruit, Dave Ridings, bagging a brace on his debut. Seven days later, down at the Shay, another Ridings double brought us back from 0-2 down to Northampton to earn us a point. This was our purple patch. But there it ended.

Once again, defeat followed defeat, except for, wait for it, our third and last home win of the season in February, when we beat Lincoln 2-1. Typically, I was away and missed it. The next time Town would win at home was a 6-0 hammering of Telford in the Conference the following October (I would miss that as well). Believe it or not, in missing just those two matches, I actually went a full year without seeing Town win at home!

When we needed everyone to pull in the same direction, the board, who had told us in December that they would at least see the season out, elected to sell our best players. Paul Wilson went to Burnley, Linton Brown, who had arrived mid-season, went to Hull, Jimmy Case moved to Wrexham (and ended up getting promotion). Then, to top the lot, leading goalscorer Ian Thompstone was sold to Scunthorpe before transfer deadline day. What the hell was going on? Did we really think that the likes of Jason Hardy, Kevin Megson and David German – however promising he might have been – were going to get us out of trouble?

It was at this point that our local paper, the *Evening Courier*, latched onto the seriousness of Town's situation. In March they launched a 'Staying Alive' campaign, in a futile effort to stem the tide. We were pleased at long last to see the *Courier* doing something positive on Town's behalf, because we were getting sick and tired of them filling the back pages with useless information regarding the enemy, Halifax Rugby League Club. The *Courier* printed coupons so that fans could gain cheaper admission, and urged local businesses to support the team. Everything culminated in a carnival atmosphere created for Town's home game with Shrewsbury Town on 20 March. We had balloons, the Friendly Brass Band, and a pre-match fireworks display courtesy of some bloke from Huddersfield (mind, it hardly worked – fireworks in broad daylight generally don't work ... all we got were a series of loud bangs). When skipper Billy Barr launched his own rocket from fully 35 yards to put Town ahead, the swollen crowd (the gate was over double that of the previous home match) must have thought we were on a home banker. But typically, as it had been happening all season at the Shay, the visitors were allowed a soft equaliser, and the game ended in a draw.

Defeats by Chesterfield and Wrexham saw us drop to the bottom of the table for the first time, and suddenly the results of fellow strugglers Torquay, Gillingham, Hereford and Northampton were as important as ours. In an effort to turn things around, Rathbone gave us Peter Craven (not a bad player, but raw at this level), Nicky Everingham, and (later) Nigerian Godfrey Obebo, who had been on the books of Bury. Rathbone later admitted he knew little about Obebo, but he was in a desperate situation. He may have been desperate, but Obebo, a comical-looking figure, never actually started a game for us, although we won on the day when he made his debut for us at Doncaster. A further win at Bury gave us hope of survival, but when Walsall coasted to a 4-0 win at the Shay, all the frailties of our side were fully exposed and things looked bleak.

In our penultimate game we travelled to Gillingham. At this point they were as desperate for the points as we were, but two long-range strikes after we had defended doggedly ensured their safety. We had come to D-Day, our last game being against Hereford. Unfortunately, it was to be at the Shay. And we just couldn't win there.

The *Courier* drummed up more support, local television came down to interview the fans, and Rathbone motivated his players for what, for most of them, would be their biggest match. For months he'd been saying the players didn't know how lucky they were to be playing in so many cup finals. Now, here was the biggest of them all. But if playing at the Shay was a handicap in itself, so too was the fact that Town's fate was not in their own

Goalmouth action against Hereford in the final League game. (Photo: Keith Middleton.)

Battling in the final game against Hereford. (Photo: Keith Middleton.)

hands. Not only had they to beat Hereford, they also had to hope that Shrewsbury could beat Northampton at Gay Meadow, as they were the only team that Town could overhaul.

The fans were expectant, though there must have been a good few in the bumper crowd of 7,451 that had come to watch Town's seventy-two-year-old Football League membership come to an end. Personally, I felt that we only needed a goal, reckoning that Shrewsbury would beat Northampton as they were still fighting for a play-off place. But that was our trouble, you see. We just couldn't score. Dave Ridings missed a sitter early on, and by the time the next real chance came along in the second half we were a goal down.

The game itself was hardly a classic. These were two poor teams, but at half-time it was still 0-0, and we had the good news that Shrewsbury were 2-0 up over Northampton. Just one goal therefore, was all we needed here. Surely, it wasn't too much to ask? But then, just after the hour, Derek Hall, a former Town player, side-footed Hereford into the lead, and Town's misery was almost complete. I remember the mood distinctly changing. All optimism of Town surviving filtered away when news came through that Northampton had stormed back at Shrewsbury and were now leading 3-2. A huge roar from the Skircoat Shed tried to lift the players. I rushed off to the loo to empty a bladder that had taken in a huge amount of Worthington's to brace myself for the occasion. When I returned to the Shed, there was an eerie atmosphere. We knew the ghost was up. Rathbone sent on striker Nigel Greenwood for young full-back David German, and he promptly squandered three good chances. But it wouldn't have made any difference.

Northampton had to lose anyway, and they hadn't. The final whistle went and it was all over.

The players headed for the dressing room. Halifax born and bred Billy Barr was carried shoulder high by supporters as if he was a sporting hero. I suppose in some way he was to those who carried him, as he felt the pain of relegation every much as each of those true supporters who had followed the club through thin and thinner.

The players re-emerged later to speak to us, the fans who had gathered by the tunnel. 'We'll be back,' sang the fans, while certain players such as Lee Bracey and Chris Lucketti proclaimed much of the same. Chairman Jim Brown came out to speak to us and offer some hope. Most fans applauded him, though there was one lone voice that insisted on shouting out, 'It's all your fault.'

So where did the problem really lie? Well, some reckon it went as far back as 1976 when the popular Johnny Quinn was axed. For me, it was just poor management of the club through a succession of chairmen, directors and managers. Somewhere along the line, someone should have been prepared to speculate to accumulate. Sam Rourke, chairman between 1981 and 1982, perhaps had the best chance, but he threw his money into ground security and club facilities when the team should have been the priority. When the end came, though, Jim Brown was adamant that the club would do all they could to regain League status at the earliest possible opportunity. Manager Mick Rathbone escaped from any criticism, simply because he was such a nice guy. He gave it his best shot, but it hadn't been good enough. It was just unfortunate for him that he should appear to be the fall guy when much of the damage had been done over the years leading up to this.

Nobody was under any illusions, despite the promises made by the club, and promotion at the first time of asking never looked likely and certainly not with the players we had then. In any case, Halifax Town's success rate since formation in 1911 hardly suggested that Town would be up there challenging from the off. In fact there were many, myself included, who thought Halifax Town would never see League football again. Lincoln, Darlington and Colchester United – the first two after only one season – had regained their place in the League by winning the Conference. They made it look quite easy. For Halifax Town, well, it just wasn't going to happen. Or so we thought. Looking back now, you could call it five years in the wilderness. Actually,

in some respects, Conference football was quite an enjoyable experience. But there was always this lingering thought that we were missing out on the real thing.

The five years we spent in the Conference were anything but a rollercoaster. Peter Wragg, appointed in favour of Mick Rathbone (who reverted to his old job of physiotherapist), gave us our biggest day since victory over Manchester City in the FA Cup in 1980. In front of the Sky cameras we defeated West Brom 2-1 in the FA Cup, but Wragg himself was gone by February, sacked through failure to deliver in the Conference. His successor, John Bird, went close in our second season, but by the end of that Halifax Town were close to closure thanks to a £30,000 tax debt. John Stockwell had taken over as chairman in March 1995 when Jim Brown had left the club (after the Council had failed to agree to selling the Shay in order to finance redevelopment at Thrum Hall, home of the rugby club). Stockwell was left to pick up the pieces, but in the event it was the fans who miraculously dipped into their own pockets to raise over £15,000 and help save the club they loved.

Bird left in March 1996 following defeats of 0-7 and 1-6 at Macclesfield and Kidderminster respectively, and George Mulhall, who had returned to the fold as youth coach, took over on a temporary basis along with Kieran O'Regan, Bird's finest legacy. He had brought the former Brighton, Huddersfield, West Brom and Republic of Ireland international to the club at the start of 1995/96, and O'Regan proved to be one of the club's finest ever players, scooping the Player of the Year award that season. We all hoped Kieran would be given the job full-time, but prior to Town's penultimate game of the season, at Woking, the players – and O'Regan – were introduced to the man who had been chosen by the board to revive Town's fortunes. This was John Carroll, the former Runcorn boss, who had been sacked at Canal Street earlier that season following a 0-8 home defeat by Stevenage.

With the glories of the Conference-winning campaign still lying ahead, people forget that the chairman who took a lot of praise for that success, John Stockwell, was also responsible for bringing Carroll to the club. It was an appointment that nearly killed Halifax Town and almost saw the club tumbling out of the Conference into the Unibond in 1996/97. The fans revolted as Carroll's reign gave us some of the club's most embarrassing moments, such as a 1-4 home defeat by Bishop Auckland in the FA Cup, and a 1-2 defeat, also at the Shay, by the mighty Harrogate Railway in the West Riding County Cup.

Had Carroll stopped on another game after losing 4-5 to Bath City in February 1997, the fall into the Unibond would have been unavoidable. I say this with confidence, because after Carroll had left Stockwell once again turned to Mulhall and O'Regan, Town won their next three matches, and these ultimately saved the club from an unthinkable relegation. But it went to the wire. In a scenario that almost mirrored that of when Town were relegated from the League, Town had to win their last match at home to Stevenage. Anything less and a win for Bath over Northwich would have meant Town's drop into oblivion.

As it happened, Bath came back from 0-2 down to lead – and win – 3-2, and that news filtered back to the Shay, where, with the minutes ticking away, Town led, having been twice behind, by a similar score. Mick Norbury (subsequently sold to Hednesford) was the hero of the hour, scoring a hat-trick, but it wasn't until Geoff Horsfield popped up with Town's fourth in injury time that we could rejoice.

On the eve of the 1997/98 season, the bookies looked at us and offered us odds at 66-1 to win the Conference. For those Town fans who always fancied a flutter whatever they felt about our chances, it was one of the best day's work they ever did. Fortunately we had George Mulhall back at the helm, and we all knew he was a wily old fox. He'd been at the Shay back in the 1970s, masterminding the mother of all great escapes in 1972/73, when Town won their last four matches to avoid the drop into the old Fourth Division. The following year Town finished a remarkable ninth on a shoestring. He left in September 1974, but resurfaced at Bolton Wanderers and Bradford City. John Bird had brought him back to Halifax as youth team coach in May 1995, and now Mulhall was being given the scope to do things his way.

Mulhall knew what was needed, and brought the players to the club that could play the way he wanted. They included goalkeeper Lee Martin, who came in for Andy Woods, and wing-backs Andy Thackeray and Mark Bradshaw. Mulhall then turned to an old friend from his Bradford days, centre-back Peter Jackson, knowing he could get the players going. Just when we thought our team was settled, Mulhall brought former favourite Jamie Paterson back to the fold. Paterson had been part of the side that was relegated in 1993, but had left the club during our second Conference season for unproductive spells with Falkirk and Scunthorpe United. We all knew his affinity lay with Halifax, and we were delighted to have him back.

The side clicked practically from day one and a 2-1 victory at Hayes was the best of starts to a great season. Horsfield, who the previous season had struggled to dislodge Norbury from the side, arrived hot off the building site to net the opener, with Lyons getting our second. We hardly looked back. Due to the pitch not being quite ready for the start of the new season, our first three matches were all away from home, but Town came through unscathed, and waited patiently to dispatch Welling 1-0 at the Shay on 30 August. When we won 3-0 at Telford, Mulhall couldn't help but praise his side after witnessing one of the finest exhibitions of football a Town side had ever put on. On Friday 5 September, in a game brought forward because of the funeral of Princess Diana, Town beat Yeovil 3-1 to go top of the Conference, and looked good to stay there.

With Horsfield scoring for fun, Town won eight games on the bounce to stay ahead of the field, with Morecambe in hot pursuit. When the two sides met at Christie Park, over 1,000 Town fans made the journey to swell the gate to 3,940. How times had changed. The previous season, this fixture was watched by just 711. Town lost then by a single goal. This time they played well for a draw and would surely have won had O'Regan not been unfortunate enough to deflect Shirley's cross over Lee Martin for an own goal.

Town's good run in the qualifying rounds of the FA Cup meant they lost top spot, but had games in hand. It was in some way almost a relief when we bowed out at Gainsborough, but having scored thirteen goals in the first three rounds to see off Droylsden, Leigh RMI and Ossett Town we knew we were now in a class of our own against non-League opposition.

Statistically, we were looking good in the Conference, but statistics have a habit of not telling the whole truth. Peter Jackson, organising the defence as well as anyone could and with the experience of seventeen years in the game, left to take up the vacant manager's job at Huddersfield Town, one of his former clubs. He had played just eight Conference games for us, but the part he played was absolutely vital. How we would miss the way he waved his shirt in front of the Skircoat Shed after each home victory (as each one was when he played). We all wondered how we would manage without him, then George Mulhall had a good slice of fortune. A plumber he knew was working for former Coventry and Newcastle hard man Brian Kilcline, and told George that 'Killer' was out of the game having been released by Mansfield Town in the close season. Mulhall took the opportunity and brought 'Killer' to the Shay, and, with Jamie Murphy arriving shortly afterwards, Town kept things rolling along.

Murphy slotted in at sweeper, Stoneman and Kilcline won everything in the air, while Thackeray and Bradshaw spent as much time in the opposition's box than they did their own, so much did Town go forward. When we lost Horsfield through suspension, the young Darren Lyons came in and did a man's job. Horsfield returned a week after Stoneman's headed goal at Stalybridge had regained us top spot in the league, and responded in typical fashion by netting a hat-trick against Hereford.

Town's twelve-game unbeaten start to the season had already come to an end by then. Cheltenham, in the Conference for the first time but having come from the other end, would go on to be runners-up to Town, but when they beat us 4-0, serious questions were asked. The football Town served up after that, however, showed that it was just a blip, and even when we lost at Leek on 13 December, the opposition were completely outplayed.

The defeat at Leek did, however, precipitate a mid-season crisis, which saw Town go four games without a win. But still we held off the challenge of Cheltenham and Rushden, and returned to winning ways on New Years'

'Killer' Kilcline heads clear against Hednesford. (Photo: Keith Middleton.)

Day against Gateshead, now managed by John Carroll. He must have been smiling on Boxing Day when his side came back from 0-2 down to earn a share of the spoils at the International Stadium, but a brace from Horsfield this time more than redressed the balance.

Perhaps sensing that Town might just hold on to top spot and claim the Conference title, chairman John Stockwell knew that we would never get back into the Football League with the Shay ground in its present state. From January, the club was fighting two battles, one on the pitch, the other off it, as the derelict Trinity Garage end was transformed into a brand new stand, that would meet Football League requirements. No matter what we did on the pitch, if the ground wasn't up to scratch we wouldn't be returning to the League.

The deadline for completion was 31 March – previous winners of the Conference, Kidderminster, Macclesfield and Stevenage, had been denied Football League admission because their ground was not ready by the then deadline of 31 December – and Blakedell Construction began work on 5 January. I must admit that whilst Halifax Town were doing their bit on the pitch, there were times when I really wondered if it would all be in vain as the deadline fast approached.

As we went into February, Town held a ten points lead, but their next game was away at fourth placed Rushden. The game saw the only start that season by 'keeper Andy Woods, but even he couldn't be blamed for all four goals that Town conceded. In fact, we were lucky to escape with four, so much were Rushden dominant. As we got back on the supporters' coach after the game, arguments ensued as some convinced themselves that Town were blowing up.

Fortunately this was not the case. Town simply responded by winning their next three matches and, following two draws, hammered Morecambe 5-1 at the Shay to set themselves up nicely for the return visit of Rushden on 21 March. By now, the footballing media were waking up to the fact that Town were realistic challengers for the title. Well, more than that, we were actually the favourites. The game over Rushden would prove this once and for all. Town absolutely pummelled Rushden, in much the same way that they had done to us the previous month. The scoreline may only have been 2-0, and the opener may have been an own goal by Wooding (under pressure from Kevin Hulme) as late as the 72nd minute, but Rushden knew that it could have been a lot more. Jamie Paterson sealed victory in the 85th minute when he latched on to Mark Bradshaw's rolled pass, rounded the 'keeper and slotted the ball home from twelve yards out. The Skircoat crowd went wild, and after the final whistle, when all the cheering had died down, there was a hum on the terracing as folk turned to one another in some sort of shock at what they had just witnessed. Nothing was going to stop us now.

And so it turned out. When the Football League came to inspect the new North Terrace on 2 April, and duly gave their nod of approval, it was a question of when, and not if, Town would wrap up the Conference title

Geoff Horsfield sees his shot saved by the Rushden 'keeper. (Photo: Keith Middleton.)

The completed North Stand terrace – League requirements met on time. (Photo: Keith Middleton.)

and claim their regained Football League status. Mulhall had been forced to call upon 'keeper Phil Morgan for the Rushden game because of an injury to Lee Martin, but when his club Stoke City recalled him, Mulhall turned to Andy Rhodes and took him on loan till the end of the season from Airdrie. Rhodes, a real character and popular with the fans, would play a vital part in the final run-in.

The new terracing was used for the first time against Woking on 4 April and a solitary strike from Hulme put us an incredible thirteen points clear. At Hereford seven days later, a backs-to-the-wall performance earned Town a goalless draw, and on Easter Monday at home against Southport they showed their true spirit by coming back from 2-3 down and with only ten men (following O'Regan's sending-off) to win 4-3, sub Dave Hanson the hero of the hour by netting two late goals to turn the game on its head. Now, victory at Kidderminster in the next game would confirm Town as champions.

Whether he actually said it or not, or whether the *Evening Courier* was playing it up rather more than they should have done, Kidderminster's secretary Roger Barlow's claim that Town 'won't win the title here' acted as the perfect spur for the Shaymen ... and the fans. They travelled down to Staffordshire in their hundreds – over 1,000 in fact made the journey – and we were treated to scenes the like of which we had never before witnessed.

In the social bar before the game, the Town supporters claimed the tables and chairs down both sides of the hall, and when a few starting chatting

'Champions', it was picked up and soon the whole of the club was reverberating as the visiting fans sang their hearts out. In the ground, it was much the same, but there was one heart-stopping moment when Kilcline upended Mike Bignall to concede a penalty. Within seconds, however, we were all singing again as Andy Rhodes got down to turn away Ian Arnold's kick and keep the game alive. Three minutes before half time, 'Super Geoff' (Horsfield) latched on to a miskick by 'keeper Steadman to put the Shaymen ahead, and in the second half there never seemed any concern that we were going to throw the game away. Then, with ten minutes remaining, Jamie Paterson cut in from the left and unleashed a shot with his unfavoured right foot from 25 yards that beat the 'keeper at the left-hand post and we were 2-0 up and claiming the title.

The final whistle went and the fans poured onto the pitch to salute the heroes who had given us our finest ever season since promotion to the Third Division in 1969. Jamie was hoisted high and carried to the tunnel, clearly in tears, so overcome with emotion was he. He had been the only one, apart from the fans, who had been there when we were relegated, and now his goal had helped clinch the title. We were back in the League and still had three games to play.

The fact that we failed to win them is almost academic. The players, somewhat understandably, failed to motivate themselves for the trip to

Happiness is a cigar called ... (Photo: Keith Middleton.)

The champions celebrate. (Photo: Keith Middleton.)

Northwich two days later. The Northwich players formed a guard of honour as the Shaymen took to the field and Queen's 'We Are The Champions' blared out. But Town didn't play like champions and lost 0-2. Town also failed to win their last home game of the season, but in drawing 1-1 with Cheltenham Town we did at least preserve our unbeaten home record – and that was a first. The Conference trophy was presented to the players after the game, and they milked the accolades for all they were worth. And why not? The supporters were doing much the same. This was, after all, the first time we'd come first in anything of any note since 1911.

Town's last game in the Conference was at Welling and it was a strangely subdued side that took to the field. We were humbled 2-6, and many of the fans felt hurt at the attitude of the players. It later transpired, or was it just a rumour, that there had been wranglings over new contracts, especially in the case of young Noel Horner, who hadn't been offered one and was told he had to earn one. Horner couldn't do anything right that afternoon, and the some fans got on his back. My most vivid memory of that afternoon was of Geoff Horsfield hurling abuse at a section of the supporters, and not of his goal (which took his Conference tally to 30 to earn him £1,000 as top scorer, one ahead of Rushden's Darren Collins).

There was already a feeling that things weren't quite right. Two days after the Cheltenham game, Town paraded the trophy on an open-top bus through the town as they headed to the Town Hall for a civic reception.

Jubilant fans salute the team outside the town hall. (Photo: Keith Middleton.)

The club had announced a new sponsorship deal with the Nationwide Building Society, and the bus was decked out with their banners accordingly. This upset director Chris Holland, whose firm of decorators was still the club's present sponsor. A row ensued and he resigned. Reserve coach Dave Worthington also quit after he claimed he had not had an official invite to the civic reception. Within weeks, chairman John Stockwell had also stepped down and Holland returned as chairman – but with the return of Jim Brown to the board and the arrival of his brother-in-law Peter Butler as coach before the start of the new season, the problems were just beginning. Days before the opening game at Peterborough, manager George Mulhall went 'upstairs' for Kieran O'Regan (who had never got on with Butler) to take over. Politics were taking over and the harmony of the Conference season soon disappeared.

But whatever ensued, no one could take away from us just what a marvellous time the players, the club and the fans had had during 1997/98. By the end of it we had gained over 4,000 extra fans and we all had a terrific time. Would we ever see the like again?

Jamie Paterson holds the Conference Trophy aloft. (Photo: Keith Middleton.)

From Hell and Back
(Hereford United)

Ron Parrott

1996/97   Bottom of Division Three and relegated to the Conference
2000/01   Eleventh in Nationwide Conference

As a football-mad youngster, I was never amongst the ranks of the Spurs, Liverpool, Leeds and Manchester United fans. As far as I was concerned, there was and always will be, only one United – my beloved Hereford United. I was introduced to Edgar Street by my grandfather, who was chairman of the Supporters Club and sports reporter for the local paper, at the tender age of three and I soon became addicted. Whilst the advent of *Match of the Day* and ease of travel in the early 1960s tempted youngsters away from their local teams to the more glamorous 'big boys', I never fell into this category and remained faithful to the Lillywhites, suffering loads of abuse along the way. Hereford who? What league are they in? I just smiled at them and said, 'One day, we'll meet you lot on equal terms and then we'll see!'

The 1960s came and went and no honours were won but a few more giant-killing exploits were notched up and then, at last, the football world started to take Hereford seriously. The legendary 'Gentle Giant' John Charles came to Edgar Street as player-manager and built a championship threatening side that Colin Addison inherited and refined into the most famous FA Cup giant-killing team ever. Who could ever forget Ronnie Radford's blockbusting pile-driver equaliser against the mighty Newcastle United and Ricky George's incredible winner in extra time? Hereford had hit the big time at last and my mickey-taking pals were queueing up for tickets for the fourth round tie against West Ham. The rest is history. United fought a brave draw at Edgar Street before going under to Geoff Hurst's second most famous hat-trick in the replay. Admission to the Football League followed at the end of that momentous 1971/72 season and, in front of massive crowds the following year, United finished as runners-up to Southport and shot straight up into the Third Division. Colin Addison consolidated our new-found status before John Sillett took over the reins and led United to their greatest ever season in 1975/76, when they walked away with the Third Division championship, finishing six points clear of rivals Cardiff City and leaving Millwall, Brighton and Crystal Palace trailing in their wake.

The one and only season in the Second Division, today's Division One,

Graham Turner. (Photo: Worcester Evening News.)

was a great disappointment to most and sadly, at last, the bubble had burst as United slipped straight back down into the Third. But to me, that season was a dream come true. At long last, Hereford United was playing on equal terms with teams like Wolves, Chelsea, Forest, Southampton and Blackburn and I was a proud man.

The slide continued, however, and United soon found themselves back in the basement. Many mediocre and often wretched seasons followed and United even had to suffer the ignominy of having to apply for re-election on three separate occasions. Further success was long overdue and when Graham Turner guided United to the play-offs in 1995/96, supporters thought that the corner had been turned at last. How wrong could they be? Hereford lost out to Darlington, but with the fans expecting promotion, the next season couldn't come quickly enough.

Turner was under severe financial pressure and during the close season was forced to make decisions that tolled the death knell for United's twenty-five years of League football. Steve White, scorer of almost half of Hereford's goals the previous season, was allowed to leave for rivals Cardiff City and our stalwart pivot, Tony James, went to newly-promoted Plymouth Argyle. Key midfielder Richard Wilkins returned to one of his previous clubs, Colchester United, and, to cap it all 'keeper Chris MacKenzie would be sidelined all season through injury. I have always been a great believer in the strength of a side lying down the centre of the field and, in effect, these moves meant that United had lost their goalie, their solid central defender, their most influential midfielder and most prolific striker. The writing was on the wall. I'd only just got over the disappointment of missing out on promotion last May and, already, any thoughts of another successful campaign appeared to have been thrown away before a ball had been kicked. I remember thinking to myself, 'I hope the club have got some class replacements lined up.'

After only seven games, I had my answer. United found themselves anchored at the foot of the table, with just one victory and only two goals scored. Graham Turner reluctantly had to admit that he would have loved to have kept at least two of his key players, but he maintained that financial restrictions forced him to adopt a more rigid wage structure that was more realistic for a club of Hereford's size. He insisted that the measures were essential to guarantee the long-term future of the club. 'Rubbish!' responded the fans, 'there won't be a long-term future if we lose our League status.' A general feeling of gloom and despondency descended on Edgar Street; fans knew that they were in for a long hard season.

Confidence reached rock bottom when United were drawn against Middlesbrough in the Coca Cola Cup and were hammered 7-0 in the first leg, with Italian international Fabrizio Ravanelli scoring four times in the

A final taste of the big time with a League Cup match versus Middlesbrough. (Photo: Worcester Evening News.)

An easy stroll for Middlesbrough. (Photo: Worcester Evening News.)

rout. The Northerners rested many of their stars for the second leg at Edgar Street, but still managed to canter to a 3-0 victory against a gutless Hereford side. A 10-0 aggregate defeat should not have been allowed to happen. Where was the cup-fighting tradition of old? These players were supposedly better footballers than the non-League giant-killers of the past, but they were sadly lacking in the key ingredients of determination and spirit. I felt ashamed.

Turner knew that his team simply wasn't good enough, but felt that his young and inexperienced squad could only get better. He praised them publicly and reckoned that he'd never worked with a better crew in terms of attitude and honesty. Unfortunately, it didn't show where it mattered most – on the pitch.

Surprisingly, things did pick up for a while. Rochdale were beaten 3-0 and Brighton took over the dreaded bottom rung. A second victory followed and the fans at last had something to cheer about, but this was followed by a draw and yet another defeat before they had to travel to Brighton to face the Seagulls in what was a massive six-pointer. Brighton were awful and United not much better, but an Adrian Foster goal secured all three points and Hereford's first ever victory at the Goldstone Ground. The home fans were so disgruntled that they staged another walkout fifteen minutes from time in protest at chairman Archer's running of their club. Two more victories quickly followed, including an impressive win at the Deva Stadium, where Chester City had thus far not been beaten all season. Brighton were left hopelessly behind at the foot of the table and seemed doomed to relegation when their plight worsened as a result of two points being deducted by way of punishment for pitch invasions.

At the end of October, United lay in a mid-table position, with 20 points, the play-offs within their reach and Brighton, everyone's favourites for the drop, had accrued only 9 points which were reduced to 7 following their misdemeanours. Tragically, a run of 13 games and three months without a win saw United slump to twenty-third place, with only Brighton standing between them and the unthinkable Vauxhall Conference. During this disastrous spell, three matches were drawn and ten lost, most of them by a single goal. Some supporters were calling for Turner's head, but he couldn't really be blamed for glaring errors by supposedly experienced and professional players.

Seven games without defeat, however, saw the team haul themselves back up to the relative security of twentieth place, but a lack of striking power saw point after point needlessly thrown away. Exeter City, at that time the poorest side in the Third Division, managed to turn us over at home, and defeat at Northampton a week later cast Hereford well and truly back into the relegation dogfight.

The most impressive performance of the season undoubtedly came in the next match at table-topping Carlisle United. The Cumbrian side raced into an early two-goal lead and Hereford looked doomed again, but an Adrian Foster hat-trick clinched a fantastic victory against all the odds. I was privileged to witness the game and remember being so proud to see a United side displaying real guts and determination for arguably the only time that season. I motored home a happy man, oblivious to the tedium of the 250-mile journey – surely we were safe now?

Sadly, as one swallow doesn't make a summer, one glorious victory doesn't make a rejuvenated team. United were simply dire in the next match against Doncaster and lost 1-0. Over Easter we picked up only two points; Brighton picked up three and moved ominously nearer. With only five games to go, United were now only two points ahead of the Seagulls and level on points with Hartlepool. Doncaster and Exeter were a further three and five points ahead respectively. Hereford and Hartlepool both had three home games to come whilst Brighton had only two and, to add extra flavour to the scenario, Hereford's final match was to be at home to Brighton. Surely it wouldn't come down to this? Even the game of football couldn't be that cruel.

A week later it was all smiles again and it looked as if the showdown shoot-out had been avoided. United picked up three points in a slender 1-0 home win over Colchester. Doncaster and Hartlepool also won, but that didn't matter because Brighton lost 1-0 at Scunthorpe and, with only four games remaining, the gap between Hereford and Brighton had stretched to five points.

But in the space of seven days the picture had changed yet again. United secured a point at Scarborough, Exeter also drew, whilst Doncaster and Hartlepool both lost again. But the result of the day was without doubt Brighton's 1-0 win over divisional leaders Wigan Athletic and, with only three games left, six points covered the bottom five teams. Fans from all five clubs shared the same feelings of dread. Personally speaking, I found it very difficult to concentrate on anything at all, as the situation preyed on my mind constantly. The last time I had been on tenterhooks like this was in June 1972, waiting for the vote to take place to decide whether United had been successful in their application for Football League status. How times had changed.

Torquay provided the opposition at Edgar Street for the next game and you could have cut the tension with a knife. When the Devon side scored on the stroke of half time, the groans could be heard across the Welsh border and although United fought back to scrape a draw, they could not conjure up the one extra goal that would have secured two more precious points. At ninety minutes, all ears were on the radio eagerly awaiting the other scores. Doncaster had drawn – great, at least they hadn't pulled away. Exeter were hammered 4-1 at Northampton and remained in the equation but Hartlepool had got a last-minute winner at Darlington and thus virtually secured their League place for next season. What about Brighton? We were like cats on a hot tin roof until eventually the news broke that they'd drawn as well – it could have been worse.

With only two games to go, still any one of five teams could have faced the dreaded drop but with United losing 2-1 at Orient and Brighton beating Doncaster 1-0, the candidates were whittled down to only two. The cliff-hanger, looming hypothetically for so long, had at last materialised. Brighton had yanked themselves off the bottom for the first time since October, swapping places with Hereford, knowing that a draw at Edgar Street would guarantee their League status. Hereford's task was equally straightforward: Win or bust! All or nothing! Football League or Vauxhall Conference!

Bottom of Division Three with one game to go:

Exeter City	45	12	12	21	48	71	48
Brighton HA	45	13	9	23	52	69	46★
Hereford United	**45**	**11**	**13**	**21**	**49**	**64**	**46**

★ 2 points deducted for failing to control a pitch invasion.

The tension during the forty-eight hours leading up to the match was

The Bulls and The Seagulls battle it out for League survival. (Photo: Worcester Evening News.)

awful. My 'wife-to-be' almost became my 'wife-that-never-was', I was unbearable. I could only think of the hard-fought battle over so many years to gain League status. How would my heroes of the past have reacted to the situation my beloved club now found itself in? The answer was quite simple – they would have fought to their last breath for the cause and their guts and determination would have seen them through. Could the current team do the same? I woke up on the morning of the 'Longest Day' having slept fitfully. I felt uneasy and almost sick. Deep down, I doubted the spirit and commitment of the present squad and set off for the ground feeling like a condemned man.

The two hours leading up to kick-off was a nightmare. Even the pre-match pint seemed to match the occasion – it just didn't seem to want to go down! Finally, in front of the season's largest crowd, the whistle blew and the battle was on. We were going to do it! We knew we were a much better side than Brighton, we'd beaten them at the Goldstone and we were going to beat them again! We roared the lads on until we were hoarse. We murdered them in an unbelievably tense first half and the ball seemed to be bouncing and skidding across the Seagulls' penalty area for most of the period. A goal seemed inevitable as shots rained in from all angles and surely enough it came, admittedly as a result of a deflection from a Tony Agana cross-shot. My lungs were close to bursting, as the celebrations began and Edgar Street exploded with relief. United wasted several more glorious chances to put us all out of our misery before the break but, somehow, Brighton managed to hold out, grateful to hear the half-time whistle.

I remember feeling confident, almost relaxed. All we had to do was carry on where we left off and more goals would surely come and we'd be safe. The alarm bells soon began to ring, though. Brighton actually started to venture into our half and we were even more worried when they brought Robbie Reinelt on as substitute – he had a record of scoring against Hereford whilst with Colchester and Gillingham. The moments that followed will haunt me for the rest of my life. Andy De Bont, United's 'keeper, punted a weak clearance upfield. It barely reached the half-way line and a Brighton defender typically hoofed it aimlessly back where United's defence had ample opportunity to clear it. They didn't and Craig Maskell volleyed a drive past De Bont and the ball smashed back into play off an upright. At this point my life stood still. Surely a defender would step in and clear it? Surely the moment would pass – they don't deserve a goal, they can't score, it wouldn't be fair! As if in slow motion, the ball fell straight into the path of Robbie Reinelt, who had the simple task of slotting it into an empty net. The bottom dropped out of my world.

From there on, Brighton fall back in numbers but I don't remember much more about the game, I knew we were doomed. Even at the death, when Adrian Foster looked certain to score, I knew it wasn't going to go in – there was a feeling of inevitability about it. The final minutes were the worst of my life, I could feel a lump in my throat and the tears were started

Nightmare on Edgar Street. (Photo: Tim Colville.)

Utter dejection. (Photo: Worcester Evening News.)

to well up in my eyes. It was over. What, to me at least, had been twenty-five glorious years in the Football League was over. We had proudly left the Southern League only to be ultimately dumped into the Vauxhall Conference to face the likes of Stalybridge Celtic and Leek Town. It was almost unbearable.

The scenes at the final whistle were unforgettable. Brighton had already been docked two points for illegal pitch invasions and the authorities were taking no chances. A whole platoon of riot-clad police formed a cordon on the half-way line and were still there a full hour after the final whistle, witnessing surely the most traumatic scenes ever seen at a football match. Ecstatic, singing, chanting fans at the one end; desolate, grieving, tearful supporters at the other end. It was unreal. I sat glued to my seat in the stand, tears rolling down my cheeks. I wanted to leave but, somehow, I just couldn't drag myself away. I felt ashamed. How could something so many players and supporters had fought so long for, be given away by a bunch of so-called professionals who seemed to have so little interest in the club. I felt angry and bitter.

That momentous day will live with me for the rest of my life. Yes, Hereford are a small club but, by God, we're a very proud club and we're too big for the Conference. Like the phoenix of legend, we will rise again. We'll be back! The club's motto has been quoted many times but it was never more poignant than on that day – 'Our greatest glory lies, not in never having fallen, but in rising when we fall!' Gradually, over the close

Over-cautious policing at Hereford versus Brighton. (Photo: Worcester Evening News.)

season, the shock wore off and the stark reality of events began to sink in. We're no longer a League club and we've got to compete in the Vauxhall Conference. We won't be exempt from the qualifying rounds of the FA Cup and, worst of all, we'll get no more funding from the FA. Will there be a life after the Football League?

The answer is yes, of course there is. Darlington, Lincoln and Colchester had all lost their League status and bounced straight back so there was no reason why we shouldn't do the same. In retrospect, we perhaps approached the first season in the Conference with misplaced arrogance. We weren't going to be there long, they just had us on loan! We were soon brought down to earth with a bang though. Only two victories in the first seven league fixtures was not the stuff of championship ambitions and although we flattered to deceive on occasions, we were never able to mount a serious championship challenge.

In fact, we are now in our fourth Conference season and that phrase 'flatters to deceive' sums up our achievements to date. We have been there or thereabouts at various stages of each of the seasons, but without ever mounting a serious challenge. What about the future? Ground development or possible relocation are still our uppermost concerns and the club's financial circumstances are complicated and sometimes precarious. On the field, however, there are no doubts in my mind. We are too big a club not to get back into League football: our crowds are consistently above anyone else's in the Conference and we still have the potential. United's supporters are superb, they turn out through thick and thin and desperately deserve some success apart from the occasional FA Cup run – in fact, they demand it! There's only one United and you will see us back in our rightful place before too long. It may not be this season, it may not be next season, but it will happen ... watch this space!

Fans on the pitch after the Brighton match – Seagulls fans celebrate in the background. (Photo: Tim Colville.)

Apocalypse Then
(Brighton & Hove Albion)

Roy Chuter

1996/97 Twenty-third in Division Four
2000/01 Champions of Division Three

Having celebrated Millennium Eve for the second year running, we now know that the end of the world was not upon us. The reality is that it's actually three and a half years since the Apocalypse took place.

For Brighton fans, it happened between 1995 and 1997. This was a period which not only saw us taken to the brink of relegation to the Conference, but also saw the club brought to the very edge of extinction. The Brighton story is not just one about football, it's a cautionary tale of how a club can be brought to its knees by those who are supposed to be securing its welfare. Of how a chairman can wield such power that it can almost destroy a club, its history, its traditions, and the hopes of all who religiously follow it. But most importantly, it's the story of how fans can unite to save the thing that they love. Of how people of all ages, backgrounds and attitudes can secure the common good. Brighton was saved by supporters – not just supporters of Brighton, but through the help of fans nationwide, and worldwide.

Until the summer of 1995, Brighton & Hove Albion FC was just another run-of-the-mill, lower-division club with a recent FA Cup final past we all remembered only too well, and celebrated because we knew it would never return. We had serious money problems, but then didn't all clubs? The events of the 7 July, however, shocked us out of our complacency. The *Evening Argus* leaked the story that the Goldstone Ground had been sold to developers. We'd play at Portsmouth until a new ground could be built. Uproar ensued; there are certain things that you don't do to a football fan, and top of the list is flogging the sacred ground the club plays on and moving to the home of your rivals, forty-five miles away.

A few of us met in a pub that night, and that was the start of it, really. What followed was something none of us expected, and it was something positive. The people who met that evening had little in common apart from the Seagulls; there's always a gap between the well-to-do fans in the seats and the rough-and-ready types on the terraces, and it was no different at Brighton. There was the official Supporters' Club on one side, and the Independent Supporters' Association on the other. We represented different groups of people, and didn't have much to do with each other before then, but the partnership we quickly developed was vital – there were things that accountants and solicitors were good at, and there were things that the rabble-rousers could do. Both groups were as important as each other, and now, several years later, we work together and have respect for each other.

We were fighting against all sorts of things. Our club was a long-established local and cultural institution, and the directors wanted to treat it like a supermarket. Supermarkets can be closed without too much hassle – the people who shopped there go to the next supermarket. You can't do that with a football club. It has customers in the same way as a supermarket does, but those customers have a personal stake in what happens to the club in a way that the supermarket can never inspire.

What chairman Bill Archer did was to take on the local pride and the family histories and the memories of joy and despair and the pleasure of an afternoon with your mates and all the other things that make football about far more than twenty-two blokes kicking a ball about for ninety minutes. He took it on with the values he believed in, and to us those values seemed to be centred around sheer, overpowering greed. His company, which runs a chain of national DIY superstore, has since gone on a take-over frenzy, and that's left us with fewer places to shop; we'd never put money in his pockets. Buy it, strip the assets, sack the people, close it down; that sums up all that's bad about business in Britain.

Fans make their feelings clear. (Photo: Dan Westwell.)

Down in Brighton, we assume that everyone knows what Archer did to our club. There was a lot of publicity, or so it seemed. But when it comes to column inches, there was probably more about John Hartson's latest attempt to find a club that didn't think he was an injury-prone lumberer than there was about the struggles of a lower division club to stay afloat; and people forget, or don't realise, that what happened to Brighton could just as easily happen to their own club. So the story needs telling again, and again, and again, because we don't want anyone else to suffer as we did – not even Crystal Palace.

After the sale had been leaked, chief executive and former MP David Bellotti quickly stepped in to reassure the fans that the ground hadn't been sold, but his reputation began to fall apart as soon as it was proved that he wasn't telling the whole truth. The deal hadn't been signed, but it was as good as done; it was the first of a long line of evasive claims from the man who became even more of a hate-figure than Archer to the fans.

Through accountant Paul Samrah, we, the fans, started to look into the club's books, and that's where the big shocks came. We found out that there were no genuine plans for a new ground, and that Archer had invested the princely sum of £56.25 in the club – and had changed the club's Articles of Association so that the directors could benefit if the club ceased to function.

Of course, the FA should have spotted the change. Its rules say that every club must have a clause relating to closure, and that clause cannot benefit the directors. The old clause, in place since 1904, said that surplus funds and fittings should go to other local clubs if the Albion no longer existed. But the FA was as complacent as we were and, to a large extent, it still is. Eventually, after some of the club's fans alerted the FA to the breach of its rules, it pressured the directors to reinstate the clause, accepting the story that it had been removed due to an oversight. To this day, no member of that board has been punished, or even reprimanded, over this 'oversight', or indeed over any of the things that happened after it.

Directors of football clubs are no longer banned from the game when caught in some wrongdoing. Ken Richardson, the wrecker of Doncaster

---

"If a player gets banned for ten months for kicking ONE fan, what do you do with people who have kicked EVERY single fan a club has?" – Stuart, a Wycombe Wanderers fan

The FA's answer: Nothing.

At the end of this season Brighton & Hove Albion FC will have no ground, no money and probably no place in the Football League, all thanks to owner Bill Archer - a Blackburn-based businessman who clearly has no passion for the club or the game.

You may think that English football needs clubs like Brighton & Hove Albion. Well right now Brighton & Hove Albion supporters need people like YOU.

Please join us on February 8th, wearing the colours of YOUR club. It's not about supporting Brighton for the day. It's about supporting fellow football fans in their hour of need. It's about sending a message to the world that football belongs to the FANS.

Football is not a businessman's toy.

**Saturday February 8th at the Goldstone Ground
Brighton & Hove Albion v Hartlepool United**

FANS UNITED
...against Archer ...against corruption ...against greed

For more information on Fans United - including details of local spin-off events - visit the Albion Campaign pages at http://homepages.enterprise.net/gjc/campaign/ or call 01273 420401. To pre-book tickets (£10) call the club on 01273 778855.

Rovers, will soon be out of prison. He's there because he arranged for their main stand to burn down. He had previously organised the Flockton Grey ringer scandal, and was warned off racecourses for life. He had closed down Bridlington Town after selling off the ground. He made Donny Rovers the laughing stock of the League, with a team even worse than Brighton's in 1997/98. Have you heard that he's banned from the game? Thought not.

But I digress. Back in Brighton, 1995/96 was hell. Relegation to the lowest division was a certainty long before the season was out, and we nearly went out of the FA Cup to Canvey Island, five divisions below us in the pyramid. That was just surface material. The worst of it was that we were about to become homeless, and the slick statements from Bellotti merely made the fans distrust the board more.

The weird thing was that Bellotti seemed to love being the most hated man in Sussex. Archer stayed out of the limelight as best he could – not too difficult, as his Blackburn home was so far away – and left Bellotti to face the flak. He did more than that. Week after week, he'd sit in the directors' box and listen to the whole ground singing to him. And they weren't singing pleasant songs!

Faced with endless protests, a poisonous atmosphere at the ground, and increasing bad publicity on a national scale, the company that had bought the Goldstone offered it back to the club for a year at an extortionate rent. The board refused to accept it, and continued to set its course for Fratton

Anti-Archer and Bellotti banner. (Photo: Dan Westwell.)

BRIGHTON
WANT
ARCHER,STANLEY
AND BELLOTTI
OUT NOW!
WHEN WILL THE F.A. ACT
TO PROTECT ONE OF IT'S MEMBERS?

Park. The fans knew that the club would never come back to Sussex if it was allowed to leave – not with that board in charge. And there was little sign that the board was about to go, despite the pressure.

That was part of the problem in 1995/96. We knew who to fight against, but we had nobody to fight for. And then came Dick Knight. Dick had his hands full with the Wonderbra ads – Eva Herzigova was a discovery of his, and she sold a lot of bras. But that era had come to a close, and Dick's wife had died. He needed something to fill his time. Bill Archer provided it.

Quite what the Blackburn-based chairman of a DIY company wanted with a southern Football League club has never been disclosed. Whatever it was, it didn't involve keeping football in the county. One ludicrous plan to move to a contested site to the north of Hove was unveiled. It looked like it had been written on the back of a fag packet, and without the support of the fans, it stood no chance of success. David Bellotti supposedly knew what a successful planning application looked like. Clearly, he knew what a failed application looked like, too, as that's what he produced.

It took over a year for Dick Knight and his consortium to dislodge Archer. During that time, the fans renewed their efforts with fresh impetus. They'd won an extra year at the Goldstone by invading the pitch and smashing the crossbars, causing a vital relegation match against York to be abandoned. This sounds violent, but it wasn't. People were having picnics on the pitch. You were only in danger if you were David Bellotti, and the police had told him to stay away. Bill Archer always stayed away.

We went to visit him the following season, after a defeat at Wigan that

The only time you will see Brighton fans carry Archer shoulder-high! (Photo: Dan Westwell.)

left us at the very bottom of the League. He wasn't in, but it got us more valuable publicity. There were protests every week, all of them imaginative, most of them perfectly law-abiding. Archer still refused to deal with the consortium. Eventually, the FA was forced to act. It brought in an arbitration service, and made it clear that it would act decisively against Archer if he failed to comply with it. Yes, that's right – you've just read a paragraph that has both 'FA' and 'act decisively' in it. The process took months, and we know little of it. A confidentiality agreement was signed, and it still holds.

Let's rewind for a moment. That 1996/97 season was one of the strangest any football club has ever had. This story isn't really about football matches – they were just the backdrop to a wider battle, one that we had to win if we were going to continue to have a club to support. There were some fantastic, imaginative protests. The visit to Lancashire to demonstrate outside Archer's house was attended by scores of police – including a helicopter – plus TV cameras, radio mikes, national newspaper reporters, and anyone else with a vested interest in potential trouble-spots. What form did the protest take? Fiddle-playing and poetry readings, that's what. We worked out what the media wanted, and gave them the opposite. It gave us less publicity, but won us more respect. People started to listen.

We were the first football fans to be allowed to march through London, before a match against Fulham. We'd already marched through Brighton and Hove. We had a walk-out, fifteen minutes before the end of a home match. That hurt, but there was a bigger issue at stake than three points. We boycotted a home game. Some of us boycotted more than one home game. We had a whistle protest – thousands of us blowing whistles throughout the game – which forced the referee to officiate through hand-signals. And we had Fans United Day – but more about that later.

On the pitch, we were useless. Manager Jimmy Case, as we all agreed, shouldn't have taken the job. He may have been a hard man on the pitch, but off it he was too nice for the worst job in football. His teams were swept aside week after week, and by the time he was sacked in December 1996, we'd all accepted that we'd be in the Conference the following season. New boss Steve Gritt had other ideas, however.

Albion started to win – at home, at least. They won ten and drew two of their last twelve home games. They kept losing away, but gradually the eleven-point gap Gritt had inherited was reduced, and the same team that had suffered defeat after defeat at the start of the season began to play some quite convincing football. Goldstone crowds soared, particularly since Bellotti had been reduced to hiding behind the scenes as the stewards threatened strike action if he showed his face, which meant that the fans concentrated on supporting the team rather than attacking the man many

Protest march. (Photo: Dan Westwell.)

regarded as the destroyer of their club.

To cut a very, very long story short, by the time the anniversary of the York invasion came, the take-over was all but signed, sealed, and delivered. And amazingly, Albion had a chance of survival. They could avoid the Conference if they won the two games they had left, and other results went their way.

First, there was the goodbye to the Goldstone. An invasion had saved it once, but another one would send us down, and undoubtedly out – we'd already had two points deducted for a rather more senseless invasion, and some cretin had attacked Ray Wilkins when we played Leyton Orient. He'd aimed for the referee and missed. Doncaster were the visitors on that emotional day. 12,000 or so got into the ground – there could have been many more, but an exclusion zone had been created for self-protection purposes around the directors' box and rendered parts of the ground unusable in the process.

Doncaster players paraded around the ground with a banner before the game. They supported what we were doing to save our club. We didn't know much about their club, but maybe they were talking about Ken Richardson as well. Whatever, we remembered their gesture, and helped their struggle, as best we could, the following season. The links between Albion and Rovers fans are strong now. Albion won the game 1-0, Stuart Storer getting the goal halfway through the second half. The roar of relief when it hit the net could be heard in Blackburn and at Lancaster Gate. The

Albion take the field in the final game at the Goldstone. (Photo: Jackie Mooney.)

Doncaster Rovers players acknowledge the Albion faithful before the Goldstone's final game. (Photo: Tim Colville.)

second roar greeted the full-time whistle. The third, the most ecstatic of them all, heralded the result from Brisbane Road, where Hereford had lost and fallen below Albion. It was the first time Albion had been off the bottom in nearly six months.

The final game had to be at Hereford. Every now and then, fate provides a match where everyone in the crowd has gone there knowing in advance that, come the moment when the ref. sounds the three blasts, they'll be feeling either the impossible high or the impossible low, and in the stands and terraces at the other end, they'll be feeling the opposite.

Consider Liverpool *v.* Arsenal in 1989? Sure, they knew, those in the ground – and even those Nick Hornbys watching on telly – that there'd be ecstasy or misery at the end, and nothing in between. But if the Gunners hadn't got that second goal, their fans would have been disappointed but not devastated; it had been a brave try.

So you have to go right to the other end of the scale, to the footballing festival of fear that was Hereford *v.* Brighton in 1997, to find the ultimate extreme. One end delirious at the end of ninety minutes, the other suicidal – and it could be no other way. One of us would stay up, the other would drop to the Conference and, maybe, oblivion would follow. Hereford had to win and Brighton needed only a draw – but had the worst away record in the country.

There were 5,000 from Hereford and 3,500 from Brighton crammed into a ground planned before anyone had heard of sightlines. There was no

Expectant Brighton fans before the Hereford match. (Photo: Tim Colville.)

live TV. We had this all to ourselves, but then who else would want it? Ninety minutes with everything but good football – nervousness, apprehension, tension, passion, joy, despair, hope, fear, all equally shared; and finally, ecstasy and misery, not equally shared. A rollercoaster for the emotions; none of us wanted to be here, none of us wanted to repeat it, but none of us would have dreamed of missing it.

I was one of those in the away end, hoarse before the game started and standing on a flat area between terrace and fence where I can see all but the nearest ten yards of the pitch. The first half was terrible, and bear in mind we knew terrible football when we saw it ... we'd been watching it for months. And then the despair of conceding the first goal – can't see who scored it, even though it's at our end ... own goal, we think.

Half time brings despair mixed with relief. It could be, and should be, a whole lot worse and somehow we prepare for another forty-five minutes of believing in the unbelievable. The second half is better – still poor, but better. We're on the offensive now, and the home end's quiet. There are, however, not many chances. But then, on 65 minutes, Craig Maskell hits the post, someone in blue and white latches on to it, shoots ... and you can suddenly sense it – the net billows, and the world's exploded in the glorious light of ninety-first place in the League. Two strangers with a combined age of seventy and a combined weight of thirty-seven stone dance wildly about the flat area like lust-crazed sumo wrestlers. I'm one of them. We've equalised; Robbie Reinelt, we think.

And then the longest twenty-five minutes in history. Tension, tension and more tension followed by some frantic whistling tension ... Foster, clear for Hereford in the last minute and a gentle toe-poke straight at Ormerod (still more tension). Finally, through the cacophony, although we can't hear the whistle, we watch the ref. raise it to his lips and twirl like an arthritic ballerina in treacle with his arm aloft like Tony Adams – it's over and we're safe. Better than sex? Better than the best sex ever.

In the end, we stayed up because we scored three more goals than Hereford. On Fans United Day in February, the most moving and inspirational day many of us have ever seen, we'd beaten Hartlepool 5-0 in front of fans from countless dozens of clubs from all over England, and farther afield. That day kept us in the Football League. I don't suppose Hereford fans will agree with this sentiment, but thanks to all who came.

Robbie Reinelt: Albion hero.
(Photo: Tim Colville.)

And now? Look at the table. We're on the way up again. But it's been a mighty battle, and there's so much left to do. A disastrous board, following on from decades of unimaginative and uncaring mismanagement from previous boards, leaves a legacy that takes years to recover from. How long will it be before Doncaster make it back to the League? Will they ever do it? And how long will it be before Brighton are playing at a permanent ground in the county?

That's the main aim now, and it has been ever since the Goldstone bit the dust after that Doncaster game. Gillingham had offered a place to play, and Archer and Bellotti had accepted it. It was almost as if they had looked at a map of the south east and picked out the most inaccessible ground in the area. Gates fell alarmingly, and performances got even worse. Only that dreadful Doncaster side kept us out of bottom place.

The nightmare at Gillingham should have lasted a year at the most. The new board had tried to move the club to Millwall, and then Woking, realising that the stay at the Priestfield Stadium was so heavily associated with the hated and discredited former board that it was keeping people away. There's a lot of symbolism in football, and at the end of the day it's about pleasure. You have to be comfortable with the place your team's playing, and if you're not, you don't go. Nobody knows how many fans stayed away because Gillingham was the place Archer and Bellotti selected for us, but anywhere would be better than Priestfield.

It wasn't to be. The other groundshares fell through, and the club stayed at Gillingham. Meanwhile, the Goldstone became a retail park. Sold by Archer for £7.4 million, it was sold on by the developers for £24 million. Symbolism here, too – many of us won't shop there, or even look at the place. There are plenty of rival places to shop. It's the only revenge we can get – if the companies that take on controversial sites are hit in the pocket, maybe they'll think twice before doing it again.

The board diverted back to Sussex, and with Crawley's excellent new ground a non-starter, the only alternative was a run-down athletics track in the Withdean area of Brighton. There were problems. Withdean is one of the few areas of Brighton – as opposed to Hove – mainly populated by well-heeled pensioners. Many of them have moved to the area from elsewhere, and few have any interest in football or their local club. They put up a fight.

To their credit, Brighton & Hove Council has been increasingly supportive in recent years, and the Withdean move was approved despite opposition from the local Tories, several of whom represent Withdean. That wasn't the end of the matter. Some Withdean residents organised a pressure group, SWEAT – the Save Withdean Environmental Action Team, though quite where the environment came into their deliberations was open to question. Many of them seemed to object mainly to the lower-class oiks they suspected they'd encounter, urinating in their letter-boxes and gassing the badgers they wanted us to believe lived in the nature reserve next to the picturesque stadium. Of course, if we'd been golfers or rugger players or tennis players, we'd have been welcomed with open arms – but that's only to be expected in areas like Withdean.

Their fight was fairly successful. The whole of the 1998/99 season was spent in the Priestfield wasteland while the various legal challenges went on and on and on. But eventually, the threats were exhausted, and when the time came for Albion to play their first game at their new home – initially approved until 2001, and now extended for another couple of years to allow the application for a permanent ground at Falmer, near the universities, to proceed – the expected Volvo road-blocks and twin-set-and-pearls picket-lines failed to materialise.

Withdean will never be a real football ground, but Falmer, if it happens, will be fabulous. The plans, designed by the people who put together the Olympic Stadium in Sydney, look stunning. It won't just be a football ground – it'll be used by sporting people of all kinds, and also the universities. The piece of land to be used is a field surrounded by a 1960s university, a railway line, and two major roads. No-one could call it a Site Of Outstanding Natural Beauty, but that's what it is to us. That's because it's within walking distance of the South Downs – although, as the Albion programme recently put it, standing within half a mile of Anna Kournikova doesn't make you beautiful. And in any case, football grounds are sites of outstanding natural beauty for many people around the country.

There are numerous hurdles still to jump, including the inhabitants of Falmer itself, clones of the SWEAT group – but the Falmer project is the best hope Sussex has ever had of a place in the sporting elite. The council may not approve it; there may well be a public inquiry; the Government may call it in and reject it; there are questions about funding. But the dream can come true. Clubs that suffer financially, or from the kind of boardroom that could only be improved by a flamethrower, can survive and thrive. It takes time and commitment and hard work and determination and teamwork, but it can be done if the right people are in place.

The board at Brighton generally gets on well with the fans these days – Dick Knight comes to my flat sometimes, and I've been known to stagger in from the pub at midnight and find him nattering about football with my flatmate. We believe in him.

If you are a fan of one of those clubs that is not so lucky, or if you don't trust your club's board, the excellent book *Build A Bonfire* – the fans' story of how the battle against Archer and Bellotti was fought and won, in far more detail than this little account – gives ten handy tips:

Identify the exact nature of the problem. Find qualified accountants and solicitors from your fans who will happily transcribe accounts and legal jargon into understandable language.

Unite the wide range of supporters into a broad alliance with a broad leadership. The talents of the most vociferous supporters and the usually silent season-ticket holder are equally valuable.

Debate the developing situation openly at public meetings (as well as in smaller supporters' groups in pubs and on the phone). Try to keep the inevitable rumours to a minimum and learn to spot false information.

Communicate your concerns directly to the press, media, politicians, and the FA. Make friends with journalists.

Allow imaginative ideas for protests to develop from all sections of the support. Violence against people is bad – and bad for your cause! It is a fact that 'illegal' forms of protesting often gain the most publicity, but if you are involved in illegal action, don't get caught!

Use every conceivable means of communication including the Internet, pen and paper, posters, petitions, leaflets, slogans, radio, TV, chanting, photographs, poetry, songs – and books!

Enlist the solidarity of other fans, especially fans who have had/are having problems with their chairmen or board. Phone a Seagulls fan!

Be prepared to make large sacrifices and be prepared for your relationships to suffer. (We never said it was going to be easy!)

Never take the word of your enemy for granted – it's not true until the document is signed.

Never give up. Be brave. Whatever form of action you take, you may well feel stupid or intimidated; but it's better to do than to sit and worry. Remember the spontaneous chant from supporters of a hundred different clubs standing in Brighton's North Stand on Fans United Day: 'Football! United! Will never be defeated!'

Remember that you can make a difference. You may not have to do anything that outlandish, but your club is worth whatever you do to help and promote it. It's the rest of your life you're affecting, after all.

PHOENIX (DONCASTER ROVERS)

Bob Gilbert

1997/98   Bottom of Division Three, relegated to the Conference
2000/01   Ninth in Nationwide Conference

The 2 May 1998 was a cold, grey day. For many, many South Yorkshire people it was an especially cold, grey day – the day of Doncaster Rovers' last game in the Football League. Over 3,000 of them had made the trek to Belle Vue. All of them were angry, fearful and very upset. They had come to watch the final spasm of more than seventy-five years of Football League membership. Many had come with murder in their hearts. This was directed towards two men: Ken Richardson and Mark Weaver. In fact, this duo's antics had driven many people to such despair that they were not prepared, even on such a momentous occasion, to put their gate money into the coffers of Richardson's Rovers.

The 5 March 1999 was another cold, grey day. But for those same South Yorkshire folk it was just about the finest day they could remember. Richardson had been sentenced to four years in prison for his part in the arson that destroyed a good part of the main stand at Belle Vue. This was widely seen as justice for his crimes and justice for his systematic rape and destruction of what had once been a nice little club. There were parties. There were celebrations. There was rejoicing. This almost unseemly joy was not just confined to South Yorkshire: a man in Adelaide held a party; a man in Brazil got plastered; a couple in South Africa opened their house to anyone who happened to be passing by; a man in America went out for quiet contemplation over a solitary drink; hundreds and hundreds of Brighton & Hove Albion supporters – wonderful people – inundated us with congratulations. I went to bed to sleep the sleep of the just at the conclusion of a long, arduous and sometimes frightening campaign to rid the Rovers of this man.

Ken Richardson had bought a controlling interest in the Rovers several years earlier. He was a businessman who had made his money out of manufacturing sacks. Sacks, and gambling on the horses. In 1984, Richardson had been sentenced to a massive fine and warned off racecourses for life for his pivotal role in the infamous 'Flockton Grey' scandal, in which a ringer ran at a race in Leicester. With his interest in racing forcibly terminated, he turned his attentions to football, presiding over Bridlington Town and leading them to closure. Mark Weaver was Richardson's sidekick – a man whose sole experience in the world of football had been in the commercial department at Stockport County, yet

Ken Richardson – Doncaster's 'benefactor' turned jailbird. (Photo: Sheffield Newspapers.)

who warranted the position of general manager and, subsequently, team manager in Richardson's Rovers.

Rovers' decline under Richardson began slowly. We actually looked to have a pretty good side for a while – at one point we had the best midfield in Rovers' colours that I could recall. But soon allegations began to circulate about just where these players had come from and how transfer fees had been paid and received. And then, one night in 1995, the main stand at Belle Vue went up in flames. It didn't make much of an impact at the time, but it transpired that the arsonist, an ex-SAS man named Alan Kristiansen, was in the pay of Richardson. Shortly after starting the fire, Kristiansen had phoned Richardson, using a mobile phone, to say that 'the job was done'. He then proceeded to leave the phone at the scene of the crime! It hardly took the skills of Inspector Poirot for the trail to be traced back to Richarson and he was duly arrested.

During Richardson's time at Doncaster we had been forced to witness the prolonged death throes of a club bled dry. Managers came and went with both startling rapidity and callous brutality. Decent players were replaced by lesser men – a constant stream of non-League players and trialists. For the most part they were decent men who tried their hardest, but they were never going to be of a standard to make professional League footballers. By 1997/98 the club was long since dead – with only the agony of relegation from the League to be endured as the final ignominy.

To describe the 1997/98 season as farcical would be an understatement. In that season the Rovers let in 113 goals and scored 26. They set a new League record for the longest start to the season without a win – twenty games had passed before that unlikely event happened (you wonder what Chester City were playing at ...) on 2 December. They lost 8-0 at Leyton Orient despite the Orient having the compassion to take off their two strikers with half an hour of the game still to play. They lost 7-1 at Cardiff City when it looked almost as if Richardson's peculiar coterie of South Manchester-based players were striving to score at the wrong end (they were indeed an odd bunch – all sorts of rumours were circulating about them. What is clear, though, is that they were set apart from the rest of the players at the club). Mark Weaver even started bringing in his own pals to play. The day that Brighton stuffed us 3-1 at Belle Vue saw the first and last appearance in goal of David Smith, a neighbour of Weaver's. The Rovers were bottom of the League all season long. They ended the season with just 19 points. They were simply awful.

To make it all worse, Richardson and his henchmen and women appeared dead set on alienating the few supporters who remained. We were banned from anywhere within reach of the director's box. Indeed, we were threatened with complete exclusion from matches. We were photographed and intimidated. We were alleged to be thugs and worse. And yet, not one

The last post sounds at Belle Vue. (Photo: Sheffield Newspapers.)

Fans make their feelings known. (Photo: Tony Harrison.)

person was arrested at Belle Vue all season long. Instead, we fought within the law with all we had and we were aided by supporters from clubs of every description all over the UK and beyond. A supporter of NAC Breda organised a sit-in at a home match for us. An Orient supporter taught me how to run a website. Many, many Seagulls supporters came to our aid. They even organised 'The Heart of Football', a sort of 'Fans United 2', on Valentine's Day 1998 when the Rovers played the Albion at Gillingham. (A lovely day spoiled only by the football.)

Therefore 2 May 1998 was truly a sad, sad day. It wouldn't have been so bad if the Rovers had just been a poor team who happened to finish bottom of the League. But although the Rovers were poor, very poor, it was not just a footballing story but a story of greed – Belle Vue sits on one of the most valuable pieces of real estate outside London. It was also a story of official indifference. The Football Association and the Football League appeared totally unable, or unwilling, to police their own game. They refused to answer letters and phone calls – even those alleging, with supporting evidence, criminal wrongdoing. The League had a file over a foot deep on Richardson and his Rovers, but they simply didn't want to get involved. They claimed that as a limited company the Rovers was 'nothing to do with them'.

By the time Richardson had finally been bought out by the Westferry consortium, Rovers had been stripped of almost all their assets. Two weeks before the start of their first season in the Nationwide Conference there were no nets anywhere to be found, no manager, no coach, no balls, not even any crockery. Richardson had left the club stripped bare. There were no more than five players on the books, and two of those were juniors. Would we ever make the first fixture of the season on 15 August at Dover?

The Rovers did manage to field a halfway decent team that day at Dover. They didn't win but they looked, for the first time in two seasons, as if they might actually be capable of doing so. Westferry had appointed local hero Ian Snodin as manager. Within the two weeks allowed to him he had assembled a team that included Neville Southall, John Sheridan, Tommy Wright and Steve Nicol. Ian had publicly stated that he would love to manage his first and home town club. More importantly though, he also said he would not do so if he felt that any vestige of Richardson remained to cast a shadow over the future. Fears about the motives and control of Westferry were somewhat allayed when he accepted the job.

Southall and Sheridan quickly moved on, but not before they had shown the commitment that, all season long, made that team a thing of which dreams and memories are made. Those early games were fun. The Rovers played expansive, attacking football ... but they kept losing. It wasn't that they couldn't play; they could. It was just that the quality petered out in the

Fans congregate for the funeral march. (Photo: Ray Gilbert.)

The funeral march.

A lone fan begins the sit-in protest in the League game against Hull.

final third of the field. By early September they were bottom of the table again with one win and one draw from nine games. It got worse: the hope inspired by a three-game unbeaten run in late September faded as the Rovers lost at home to fellow strugglers Woking and Farnborough Town. In fact, the Rovers were bottom of the Conference for three long months. They were in the bottom three relegation places from 12 September right up to almost the end of January.

Despite such poor form, something odd was happening. No matter that the Rovers had won only four League games by 9 January. Supporters from far and wide were turning up in numbers unseen at Belle Vue for well over a decade. One chap came across from America to watch his team play. One guy travelled from his home in Kent to every match the Rovers played that season. A bunch of Germans came over to see what all the fuss was about. They watched us lose again, horribly, to Leek Town. But attendances went on skyrocketing. From the paltry few hundred of the previous season there were thousands of happy, cheerful and enthusiastic supporters at every single game. Other Conference clubs began to take note that when the Rovers visited, they would need extra stewards. In fact, around half of that year's Conference teams had their biggest home league gate of the season with the visit of Doncaster Rovers.

Home attendances were almost treble the average of the previous season. Seven, yes, seven, Rovers websites sprang into existence. The number of fanzines circulating was almost beyond rational explanation. All this for a recently shambolic, inept and ill-used club with a team who were then still bottom of the Conference. Why? The incomparable Steve Nicol was quoted in the local press on 28 March 1998 as saying: 'I've never been at a club like it. It's certainly an unusual club. I don't think I've heard anyone criticising anybody. We've lost games at home 1-0 when we haven't been able to score and you're coming off and they're slapping you on the back as you're going up the tunnel. At most places if you come off and you've been beaten 1-0 at home for the third time that season you'd probably get a bottle on the back of the head, but not at Doncaster. Everybody's behind you completely – it's great. And the supporters have been so good to me this season. It's been great playing here. I've thoroughly enjoyed it.'

In that quote you can deduce the secret of the Rovers and Rovers supporters. The players enjoyed themselves and the supporters were, quite simply, ecstatic that they still had a club to support. Even better, the supporters were deliriously happy with a team that tried hard, usually played nice football and was moving in the right direction. Since coming back from a 3-0 deficit at home to win 5-4 in the return match against Dover on 19 December, Rovers lost four League games out of seventeen. They won away, convincingly, at Rushden & Diamonds and the then Conference leaders Kettering. They moved steadily up the table. They even won their first senior honour for thirty years: the Endsleigh Trophy (a sort of League Cup for the Conference). They found a good steady goalscorer who attracted the likes of Wolves and Bolton to Belle Vue. They paid good money for a speedy winger with a fine reputation. There was a manic, dirty (and much-loved) centre half whose ability to outjump centre forwards several inches taller was awesome. There was a goalkeeper who just could not stop saving penalties, including two in one game. The club gave away 4,000 free packets of sweets to children at the home game against Stevenage. There were firework displays before evening kick-off matches. Children were encouraged to come along with the 'quid a kid' scheme. Most importantly of all, there was innovative and effective marketing. The amount of sponsorship money the club obtained beat the target for the season before the end of December. Replica ASICS shirts, selling for a whopping £40, sold out within days.

The results are easy to see when the record books are consulted: Rovers managed an average attendance of almost 3,500 – incredible for a club that was still in the bottom half of the table – and set a new aggregate attendance record for the Conference with three home games to go. If you troubled to go to Belle Vue you would have seen, everywhere you looked, happy, smiling faces. Defeat didn't matter any more. The bond between club and supporters was too strong. I shall never, ever, forget the night in mid-December when the Rovers played at Rushden & Diamonds in an FA Cup replay. What looked like billions and billions of Rovers supporters were going absolutely mad all night long. Even Rushden supporters were impressed with the Rovers' support that night – so much so, in fact, that they talked about it for months afterwards. We lost, but it didn't matter at all. It was just so good to actually be there. What really mattered was that the Rovers still lived. Nor shall I ever forget the announcement at half time over the Kettering PA on the Saturday following Richardson's conviction. 'A request', he said, 'for the unavoidably absent Mr Richardson – who cannot be here with us today. Here's a record by The Prodigy called "Firestarter" ...'

The very last match of the season, though, has to be the best night's football I have seen for more years than I can remember. The second leg of the Endsleigh Trophy final against a Farnborough team that, despite relegation, had beaten Kingstonian, Woking and Conference champions Cheltenham Town on the way to the final. Not only was Belle Vue packed with a stunning crowd of 7,160 spectators, but over 1,000 more were locked outside (the previous year's final attracted a crowd of not much more than 1,000 to both legs). The atmosphere, the expectation, the sheer joy on every single face that night is something I have never seen before and doubt I will ever see again. Complete strangers couldn't stop chatting to each other, reminding themselves that it was exactly one year and one day since the Rovers were at death's door as they dropped out of the Football League. I have never seen so many people all smiling at once –

Ian Snodin and the triumphant Doncaster team with the Endsleigh Cup. (Photo: Shaun Flannery.)

even my mum got in on the act! The pre-match firework display not only caught the mood but also set a section of fencing on fire! The on-pitch announcement by local businessmen John Ryan and Peter Wetzel that they had bought the club from Westferry and would be building a new stadium for the season after next made a good night even better. When Colin Sutherland scored the opening goal after 10 minutes the place exploded! The Rovers were back. We won 3-0 on the night and 4-0 on aggregate. Ian Snodin said later that lifting the trophy was as good a feeling as when he won the League Championship with Everton. His, and his brother Glynn's, smiles that night would have lit up the dark side of the moon. Every time I see their beaming faces on the match video I can't help but think how far the Rovers have come in so short a time.

Countless thousands of supporters from all over the world fought for this club. Countless supporters of other clubs chipped in with invaluable help, advice and support. But ultimately the strength of Richardson's control meant that Rovers supporters fought without hope. They fought without much in the way of resources. They fought without much media attention. But they fought all the same. They fought because they cared. As Steve Nicol said in that same interview, 'Football is not just all about big clubs.'

ROLLERCOASTER BY THE SEA
(SCARBOROUGH)

Ian Anderson

1998/99   Bottom of Division Three and relegated to Conference
2000/01   Tenth in Nationwide Conference

From the moment Scarborough secured promotion to the Fourth Division in 1987, it was always destined to be something of a rollercoaster ride. Being the first club to be automatically promoted to the League meant that, suddenly, this previously unheralded club from a small North Yorkshire coastal town was thrust into the media spotlight. TV crews visited the town, it was featured in broadsheet newspapers, and the football media eagerly awaited the first League game in August.

Scarborough's opening Fourth Division fixture couldn't have been a tougher test. A home match against one of the most famous old names in football, Wolverhampton Wanderers. Unfortunately, that game has now become synonymous with the vandalism perpetrated by the Wolves' fans that day: a roof over the terracing was wrecked and – perhaps most memorably of all – a marauding Wolves fan fell through a stand roof.

After that baptism of fire on the opening day (the final score was 2-2), you wonder how the team made it to the end of the season. They almost didn't. The financial stresses of League football nearly put the club out of business, and they were only rescued when Geoffrey Richmond (lately of Bradford City) took over as chairman. Now, although the Boro fans were happy about having a team to support, Richmond's popularity slumped dramatically when, at the start of the 1988/89 season, it was announced that Scarborough would no longer play at the Athletic Ground but the McCain Stadium instead. In a groundbreaking move, Boro would be the first team in the country to play at a sponsored ground. It was so groundbreaking – and so monumentally unpopular with the fans – that it would be another six years before Huddersfield Town became the second. After that Richmond was never popular. His situation was not helped by Boro's outlay on players being far from lavish (to say the least) throughout his five and a half years in charge.

Boro had a reputation as a cup team from their non-League days. They had won the FA Trophy three times, been runners-up once, and the FA Cup often featured them in the first few rounds. Although their FA Cup form after joining the League was notoriously bad (only once reaching the third round since 1978, and being knocked out by non-League teams in two consecutive years) they were one of the teams that the bigger clubs never wanted in the League Cup. After drawing with Southampton in one leg in 1988/89, they established themselves well and truly with a 3-2 defeat of Chelsea the following year, after a 1-1 draw at Stamford Bridge. Admittedly they were hammered 7-0 on Oldham's plastic pitch in the next round, but it was worth it.

The team was knocked out by Southampton in 1991/92, before they embarked on their breathtaking (it took our breath away anyway) run in 1992/93 in the newly re-christened Coca-Cola Cup. After knocking out Bradford an astounding 8-3 on aggregate in the first round, Boro were paired with Premiership Coventry City. The top-flight outfit went into the second leg with a 2-0 lead and were looking favourites to proceed until a 73rd minute goal from Boro. The equaliser came in the final minute, and then Lee Hirst managed to get his head on a cross to give Scarborough an astonishing 3-2 aggregate victory. Plymouth were knocked out after a replay in the third round, so – after a couple of frost-related postponements – Arsenal were the visitors on a cold and extremely foggy night in January 1993. For any other fixture the game would have been called off, but this was it – the night when Boro would account for a really big club. As it was, Nigel Winterburn's twenty-five-yard toe punt decided the game, and shattered any lingering and stupidly optimistic dreams of Wembley.

League form was never inspiring. After leading the Fourth Division for a week or two in their first season, Boro seemed to suffer from vertigo, and eventually finished twelfth. 1988/89 was the 'nearly' season: after being there or thereabouts all year, Boro finished fifth in the table and lost 2-1 on aggregate in the play-off semi-finals. The 1989/90 season, beating Chelsea aside, was a crushing disappointment. Boro finished only a few points clear of relegation and didn't guarantee their League status for the following season until late April. 1990/91 was a strange year. Boro got a modicum of media coverage due to the best choice of shirt sponsor I have ever seen. For the entire season, the side ran out with 'Black Death Vodka' on their shirts. This was the year that saw Boro set the record for the lowest ever Fourth Division attendance. On a sodden December evening, just 625 diehards/lunatics/masochists turned up to see Boro beat Wrexham 4-2. After 'attracting' three or four crowds of below 1,000, Boro somehow finished ninth, just two points from the play-offs.

1991/92 can be best described as anonymous. Playing on a pitch like a ploughed field (thanks to another of Richmond's less inspired decisions to let the short-lived Scarborough Pirates rugby league club play there), the team finished mid-table. The 1992/93 campaign saw a concerted title challenge crumble, along with a respectable home record, in the last two months of the season. 1993/94 was another 'quirky' year. Not many teams get through three chairmen in six weeks. Geoffrey Richmond had resigned for approximately twenty-four hours earlier in the season, after a dispute about entry prices. He went for good in February, to the pleasure of most of the home contingent. Dave Simpson took over, before evidently deciding that the job wasn't his cup of tea a while later, and handing over to John Russell.

1994/95 was, according to most, the beginning of the end. After sacking manager and ex-Chelsea defender Steve Wicks before the season even began (for reasons that remain unclear to this day), ex-player Billy Ayre was appointed. Boro lurched from defeat to defeat, finally hitting rock-bottom in about November. Ayre departed soon afterwards, the reins being taken up by assistant manager (and boss in many transitional periods), scorer of Boro's first League goal, and general club hero, Ray McHale. The team hauled themselves off the bottom in April and finally finished twenty-third, one place above Exeter. As it happened, finishing bottom wouldn't have meant a swift goodbye to the League as Macclesfield's ground was perceived not to be up to scratch (have the people who decide these things ever been to Blackpool or Hull?).

1995/96 was more of the same, twenty-third again, but never really with the same sense of doom, thanks to Torquay being even more inept than we were. 1996/97 began with the appointment of Mick Wadsworth as manager. He had taken Carlisle up, and got to within striking distance of the play-offs at the first attempt with Boro. We held our breath for the next year ... 1997/98 – of course it was never going to happen and we capitulated pathetically in the play-off semi-finals. But there was a sense of optimism. Would it last?

The answer was an emphatic 'no'. Many of us had a bad feeling when Anton Johnson took over as chairman after an emotionally drained John Russell sold up in the summer of 1998. Johnson was the man who had, famously, allegedly used one club's money to pay the wages at another. He is the sort of character that football fans mention in the same breath as Ken Richardson and Robert Maxwell. He had been banned from taking charge of another club. Well, that was until he took over at Boro, and proceeded to turn a team of promotion contenders into relegation candidates. Money, a commodity which has never been thick on the ground at a club which would struggle for a crowd of 2,000 even in a play-off season, seemed to vanish. Wages went unpaid, a transfer embargo was slapped on the team until affairs were sorted out and the fans went from impatient to angry to furious – to the extent of sending in death threats via the local paper.

A fans' forum was held in a Scarborough pub in December that year, attended by former chairman Russell. Russell was a popular man with the fans – one of a rare breed of chairmen that really made the effort to communicate with the supporters, even going to the lengths of an Internet discussion board. He stated his intent to wrest control back from Johnson. Control was duly wrested a while later, and Boro went into the second half of the season having been well and truly shafted, but with hopes of being

Manager Mick Wadsworth – resigned mid-way through the relegation season. (Photo: Scarborough Evening News.)

able to escape their predicament. At this time they languished second from bottom with only Hull between them and the bottom of the League.

Naturally, Hull City *v.* Scarborough in March was always going to be a crunch game. In the week leading up to the match, there was a distinct feeling of 'we can win this', ever mindful that if we did we would be one step nearer to escaping the dreaded drop. The game was widely publicised as 'one of the biggest games of the season' and many Boro fans were planning on making the trip.

Walking along the Anlaby Road in Hull on matchday, you were used to seeing lots of Amber and Black fans trooping towards the ground. Nothing prepared the Boro fans for the mass exodus that day. Given the occasionally frosty reception between Hull and Boro, we zipped our jackets up, and broke away once we got to the ground. You could hear the noise once you started to cross the car park – a loud hubbub, far above anything usually produced here; Hull had a reputation of being too large to create any real atmosphere. Climbing the steps to the away end was truly awe-inspiring. The ground was almost full and they were beginning to open the usually closed derelict terrace on the railway side of the ground.

Give the somewhat 'slimline' look of the away end at Boothferry Park, 'crunch' was the appropriate term. Boro brought more fans to that game than they had had at many of the home games that year. Hull had chosen not to make this relegation six-pointer between what were (almost) two local rivals an all-ticket affair, a decision which in hindsight bordered on lunacy. The attendance was the highest in Division Three that year, an amazing 13,500. That the game finished 1-1 was almost an irrelevance; the sheer atmosphere created by both sets of fans and the good-natured feel between them reaffirmed our love of the game.

The home match against Carlisle that followed soon after was the next relegation dogfight. In the last couple of months of the season, the Scarborough fanzine had written to several other publications, and asked the editors for their opinions as to who would go down, and who they wanted to be relegated. Of all the publications solicited, none thought Boro would, or should, go down; several thought it would be Carlisle and, intriguingly, Carlisle's fanzine failed to reply. Did they have doubts? Were they avoiding harsh reality? Who knows?

The game was once again built up by the local paper and the long-dormant publicity machine at the club awoke, and managed to attract over 2,000 fans to the game – quite an achievement at any time in Scarborough. Walking into the Shed at the McCain Stadium (it still sounds as awkward and corporate a title today as it ever did), I was amazed to hear some real noise again. We had been muted and quiet for most of the season – the loudest shouts had been in the run up to Christmas, and these had been 'Johnson out' rather than any support for the team on the pitch. We settled down for what was to be a close and tense game – or so we thought.

It turned out to be a stroll for what was the most committed Scarborough team I had seen all season. It finished 3-0 and it should have been a lot more. Once Boro got their noses in front, they were never troubled. I spent the early part of the game wondering when the first goal would come, and the period afterwards musing on how many more Boro would knock past a hopelessly outclassed Carlisle defence. The general feeling among Boro's fans, indeed Division Three fans in general, after that game was that it would be nothing short of an injustice if we were to go down. Injustice or not, by 1 May, Boro were well and truly up the proverbial creek without any means of propulsion. The long and short of it was that if Boro failed to beat Halifax Town away from home, they would be out of the League; it was as simple as that.

Unfortunately, as luck would have it, this would be the one game that I couldn't get to. Instead I had Radio York on at home, attempting to listen to proceedings at the Shay. Now, listening to Scarborough games on our local BBC radio is not easy, given their obvious preference for York City games. So it came to pass that I was sitting next to the radio all afternoon listening to York City getting beaten by some team which I neither remember and care even less about, and every now and again I was being sustained by a combination of Ceefax and snippets from Boro commentator and local folk-hero Ivan Nash at the Shay.

It's always amazing how a football fan will shout at his or her radio occasionally, as if it's going to listen, and if it did, as if it would make a blind bit of difference. Come the last five minutes, and with Boro 2-1 ahead, I was doing just that. At the final whistle, I was dancing around the room, in the knowledge that Boro had a lifeline. If they beat Plymouth Argyle in midweek, they would be ahead of Carlisle.

We were destined to beat Plymouth; it had to happen to set up the perfect final-day scenario. Boro's eleven warriors went out and completed the job, and the mood around the town changed from 'we can escape' to we 'will escape'. The feeling in the town in the run-up to the last game of the season at home to Peterborough was relayed to me by a friend, seeing as I was 170 miles away studying in Coventry. The word in the streets was all about 'the match', and whether you would be there. For once Leeds United was not 'the match' that they were on about. I called the club the morning after the Plymouth game to see whether it would be all-ticket.

'No, it's not all-ticket', came the voice on the other end of the phone, making out that it was a bizarre question to ask. I suppose it was bizarre: I'd never had to ask whether any other League game there would be all-ticket, and it just summed up the situation for me – it was totally unprecedented. I sorted out my business, gave my excuses to avoid lectures on the Friday, and jumped on a coach home. Saturday dawned, and I picked up a friend from the station, who had also decided (despite being a Wimbledon fan) that he wanted to go as well.

We parked up, having decided that the ground would fill quickly, and walked in over ninety minutes before the game began. We did the usual ritual of buying a programme (we later found out that we were among the lucky ones – the club, not expecting such a crowd, only printed 500 copies, which had sold out by 1.40 p.m. (anyone that has a decent copy now would be able to fetch upwards of £30 for it), and took our places in the Shed. The general feeling was one of optimism. Carlisle had to beat – of all people – Plymouth, and hope that Boro failed to win. Surely Boro could finish the job that day?

The game kicked off with several hundred people locked out. Despite this, the official attendance was announced as roughly 4,500. Considering the ground capacity is nearer 6,500, I prefer to think of the crowd that day as nearer the latter figure. From about 2 p.m. onwards until after the game, the fans (in particular those in the shed, who can feel proud after that afternoon) never stopped singing. In all my years attending Boro games, I have never – home or away – witnessed such an amazing atmosphere. The sheer passion on display that afternoon will surely never be repeated. The song 'Scarborough 'til we die' was belted out time and again, each time

Fans celebrate at the final whistle before news of Carlisle's late goal. (Photo: Scarborough Evening News.)

more heartfelt and rousing.

The game got underway and within fifteen minutes our hearts sank as Peterborough scored. The singing was raised another notch by the Scarborough faithful, as the team poured forward in search of an equaliser. As often happens, it came just as I was wandering towards the tea-bar a couple of minutes before half time. It has now been committed to my memory as one of those moments, where I can remember nothing of the goal itself, only the memory of the ball hitting the back of the net, and of me jumping around like a hyperactive toddler after too many sugary drinks.

The second half began with both sides pressing for the decisive goal. Suddenly, word emerged from those with transistor radios – Carlisle were one down. We cheered and celebrated as if Boro had scored. Surely we were on our way now? Safety seemed almost assured when striker Darren Roberts broke through Peterborough's defence. He only had the 'keeper to beat and he deftly chipped the ball over him ... only for it to agonisingly clip the woodwork and go wide. A few minutes later, a perfect chance was called back for offside. Then came the news we hoped not to hear – Carlisle were back on terms. We reassured ourselves that we were still safe, as long as the Cumbrians didn't get another.

At 4.50 p.m. the final whistle went at the McStad, and the fans poured onto the pitch. We were wandering round in a state of near delirium, hugging total strangers, until the tannoy crackled into life; Radio 5 Live echoed around the now silent McCain stadium. We were told there had been another goal at Brunton Park. The coverage switched to Carlisle, as the commentator regaled us of the astounding events. In the fifth minute of injury time, Carlisle's manager waved absolutely everybody forward to attack a corner. The ball was swung in, and a shot rebounded to the feet of on-loan goalkeeper Jimmy Glass, who toe-poked it through a crowd of players into the back of the net.

The final whistle went: Carlisle United 2 Plymouth Argyle 1. The awful truth dawned – Boro were back in the Conference. People sank to their knees. The picture of three grown men in bright green and red fright wigs crying uncontrollably has become synonymous with this

Fans on the pitch following the match against Peterborough. (Photo: Scarborough Evening News.)

game and, indeed, the entire season. I was sat there on the turf for five minutes or so, before the team emerged, red-eyed and downcast. Chairman John Russell took the microphone, thanked us for our support and ending with the line 'we will be back.'

Within a couple of days of this final fling in the League, it was announced that Boro would appeal against their relegation. It transpired that Jimmy Glass (who was released by Carlisle soon after – a strange sort of thank-you, even by Michael Knighton's famously unorthodox standards) had been signed after the transfer deadline. Now a loophole had been introduced earlier in the year – approved by Boro among other teams – allowing teams to sign goalkeepers after the deadline, provided that it was only to cover injuries, and that it was deemed essential. All well and good, were it not for the fact that Carlisle had sold a goalkeeper to Blackpool on deadline day, leaving them woefully short of 'keepers. Boro had two arguments: firstly, that the problem was of Carlisle's own doing, and as such a replacement should not have been allowed as they obviously thought they would have adequate goalkeeping cover until the end of the season. Secondly, Carlisle had a youth team 'keeper who could have gone in goal, thus rendering Jimmy Glass surplus to requirements. Boro had been forced to rely on a youth team goalkeeper earlier in the season, when the League decided not to let them sign a goalkeeper to cover a 'keeping crisis (due to the transfer embargo) – and this situation had not even been of Boro's own making.

However, the League (predictably) laughed Boro out of the back door. I can't say I was surprised – the move smacked of desperation (even if, as I believe, they had a genuine case), and if it had worked Boro would have kept their League place by default, which would have been a hollow victory. We remembered what John Russell had said that afternoon – 'We will be back'. We would win our place back on the field.

Relegation took a while to sink in for me. It had gone into my head, but I could barely comprehend a League season without Scarborough. It was only drilled home to me in early July when the fixture list came out, with Boro's first game at home against Yeovil Town.

Nevertheless, the summer was relatively optimistic, once we'd got over the initial shock. We realised that Boro could have a good go at winning the Conference, and certainly stood more chance of a good league position than in the Division Three. The town, considering its usually totally apathetic approach to the football team, couldn't have cared less I suspect. I occasionally wonder if the populace might secretly have rejoiced in relegation, as at least it meant the town wouldn't get filled up with riff-raff wearing Hull City or Hartlepool United shirts anymore.

The actual Boro supporters were split over whether it was better to be a big fish in a small pond or a small fish in a big pond. Would it be better to lose to Cardiff or to beat Forest Green Rovers? There are fans like me (I'd guess roughly 800 to 1,000 of them) who would still turn out if Boro were playing local derbies against Bridlington Town or Whitby; fans who would turn out to matches in the League but not in the Conference; and then finally those to whom Scarborough are a 'hobby' team, very much second-place to their 'proper' team – probably Leeds United or, worst of all, Manchester United. You'll find these people in every town, although unfortunately there seems to be a disproportionately large number of them in Scarborough. You can spot them a mile off – usually kitted out in a Premiership football shirt, often with identically dressed kids in tow – looking at you like some kind of escaped lunatic when they see your Boro shirt. I can understand this reaction when I'm in Coventry; they tend not to see too many Scarborough shirts there. But in the actual town where the team is based – honestly!

Once again there was a considerable amount of 'novelty' media coverage – the same sort of coverage of the non-League teams in the FA Cup first round each year. The main question being asked of the players and fans was 'How does it feel to return from whence you came?' Perhaps having so recently come from the Conference, the Boro fans saw League membership as more of a privilege than a right. The other teams to have been relegated from Division Three probably felt the drop significantly harder having been in the League for decades at least, and have that inherent feeling of a 'right' to be there that comes with familiarity. We just sat back and thought 'well, we're down now, we had better do something about it', and turned up to the games.

Well, most people turned up for the games: as part of my course I had a placement in a location not particularly conducive to watching Boro – Germany. Nevertheless I managed to get to several games that year. The opening game against Yeovil (one of the pre-season favourites) probably lulled us into a false sense of security. But then opening day 5-0 trouncings tend to do that; Boro were top of the table.

It wouldn't last. By the time of my last game before leaving for the Continent, Boro were fading fast, and would have faded faster were it not for a last-minute equaliser against Nuneaton Borough. Boro's fans got a distinct feeling of doom when the fourth qualifying round of the FA Cup came around. We've never been particularly illustrious in that particular competition, and had been knocked out in the previous two years at home to Whitley Bay and Leek Town. Surely it would be third time lucky? Or perhaps not. The 1-0 home defeat against Tamworth was regarded as one of the most inept performances put on by a Scarborough side.

In the FA Trophy we fared a little better, despite being taken to replays in the early rounds by the footballing 'giants' that are Stocksbridge Park Steel, and Burnham (near Slough apparently). However, the fifth round saw us played off the park by the Unibond League's Bishop Auckland. It seems we hadn't lost our knack of losing in cup competitions to teams from lower echelons of football.

The sheer apathy of the Scarborough population towards their local team showed in abundance during the season. For the April game against Forest Green, prices were slashed to attract a bigger crowd, and yet still only a mere 1,600 turned out. Fourth in the table was how it ended; there was to be no swift return to the League and Conference football beckoned for longer than most would have wanted.

The season had seen a protracted take-over bid from north-east insurance magnate and Sunderland supporter Brookes Mileson. A new era of 'openness' (his words not mine) was promised. Since then, however, whatever news Boro fans could get has been hearsay, rumours, 'insider knowledge' and whatever refined nuggets of information provided by the somewhat sycophantic *Scarborough Evening News*. On the eve of the 2000/01 season, fans were given the rather rude awakening of the true extent of Boro's financial troubles – troubles to the tune of £2 million. If you take this as a proportion of gate receipts, it comes out at around 278 games' revenue. If you applied the same ratio to say, Coventry City, the debt for the Premiership side would be an unreal £100,080,000. So Boro were in trouble.

A creditors' meeting was called for 26 August in which 75% of the creditors had to approve the arrangements to allow the club to continue even to the end of the month. Considering the creditors included a high street bank, Altrincham FC and Halifax FC, the future was far from certain. The home game against Morecambe on the Tuesday night was hardly packed (less than 2,000 showed), but was far from quiet, with cries of 'you'll never kill the Scarborough' ringing out from the fans. In reality, however, there was little they could do if the powers that be decided that it would be better for the club to come to a premature end.

A margin of 4 per cent eventually sealed the creditors' agreement that allowed Scarborough to continue in its precarious existence. The newspaper pronounced 'Boro saved' as its headline, with the following day's game against Kingstonian acting as the vehicle for mass celebration. But the club is still losing money at a rate resembling a remarkable leaky sieve: £9,000 a week is widely rumoured to be the shortfall. Striker Chris Adams has had to be sold to Orient for £25,000, less than a year after the board rejected a bid from Rushden of ten times that amount. The team exited the FA Cup at the first hurdle, going down 4-3 at home to Leigh RMI. The defence is leaking goals alarmingly, and crowds have dipped below 1,000 for the first time in ten years.

Boro's new chief executive, a man previously sacked from Middlesborough and Darlington FC, has become a focal point for the growing divide between the board and the fans. To say that Keith Agar is remarkably unpopular with a lot of Scarborough supporters is an understatement. The fans are growing increasingly impatient. The board hides behind a wall of silence, while crowds ever diminish and debts ever mount. This is not a club with good prospects.

If the team survives the season, it will be some achievement. The patience of the fans may not even last that long. The relationship between football clubs and their fans is one which needs mutual trust and communication to survive. In this respect, Scarborough is in serious trouble. The fans are willing to communicate and rebuild trust. But unless the club is willing to do likewise, then I fear for the future of football at any level in the town.

Reality sinks in. (Photo: Scarborough Evening News.)

Roy of the Rovers
(Carlisle United)

Anthony Donnelly

1998/99 Twenty-third in Division Three, escaping relegation to Conference on last day of season
1999/2000 Twenty-third in Division Three, escaping relegation to Conference on last day of season
2000/2001 Twenty-second in Division Three

Every club has it's own 'Roy of the Rovers' story. Carlisle United have two, separated by a generation and an entire League. Not just a division. The entire League; all ninety-two places.

Have a look at this table:

	P	W	D	L	F	A	Pts
Carlisle United	3	3	0	0	5	0	6
Ipswich Town	3	3	0	0	4	0	6
Wolverhampton Wanderers	3	2	1	0	6	3	5

That was how the top of League Division One looked on the evening of 24 August 1974. That's right – Carlisle were top of the old First Division. The spot that is now traditionally filled with the words 'Manchester United' (who, by the way, were relegated to make way for Carlisle during this season). Now look at this second table:

	P	W	D	L	F	A	Pts
Hartlepool	46	13	12	21	52	65	51
Carlisle United	46	11	16	19	43	53	49
Scarborough	46	14	6	26	50	77	48

That one is how the bottom of Division Three looked on the evening of Saturday 8 May 1999. Scarborough were relegated to the Conference and Carlisle, courtesy of a goal by new-found 'striker' Jimmy Glass, lived to see in the new millennium as a Football League club.

So what happened in the intervening twenty-five years or so? It is a common story, and one which can be re-told by countless football fans around the world: the story of how their once successful club slowly declines and finds a level which they'd really rather it hadn't. The most interesting chapter in the Carlisle story is the one that led to the events of 8 May 1999 (hereafter known as St Jimmy's Day) and it centres on one man. But we will come to him in a minute. First we have to get a feel for the somewhat unusual circumstances in which Carlisle fans have always found themselves.

Supporting Carlisle has never been an easy option. We are possibly unique in more ways than any one club really should be. We are the only professional football team in Cumbria since the demise of Workington. Being the 'last outpost' of football in England and possibly the most isolated club in the country, we have no natural rivals on which to focus our venom. Arsenal and Tottenham have each other. Stoke have Port Vale. Rangers have Celtic. Even Norwich have Ipswich. But Carlisle? No one. We occasionally hate Burnley; I have taken a dislike to Preston; others focus attention on Darlington or Hartlepool but, as you can tell, the good people of Cumbria cannot unite against a common foe and so that particular outlet for vitriol and satisfaction in someone else's failure always feels so diluted. We often sing the line 'no one likes' but then no one really hates us either and so we generally just get on with our lives.

But then to me that is what Carlisle United are all about – we have to all pull together and concentrate on just ourselves and what we can do.

Brunton Park. (Photo: News and Star.)

During periods of success we have become figures of hate – which is, of course, one of the best compliments that fans can pay another club (ask yourself why do you hate Man Utd?) – but during the lean years, which let's be frank have far outweighed the others, the only time that people even realise that we are there is when they are faced with a four-hour drive on a cold, wet Tuesday night for an Auto Windscreens tie.

And this is why relegation to the Conference held such fear for Cumbrian football fans. Just look at the make-up of that league. The closest thing we would have to a local derby would be Morecambe or Southport. Virtually all of the clubs are in the Midlands or further south (and we in Carlisle consider Kendal the South). Where the hell is Hednesford Town anyway?

But back to our tale. To fully appreciate the predicament we found ourselves in on the morning of 8 May 1999, we need to return to the one man I alluded to earlier and examine events from his entrance. The man to whom I am referring is one Michael Knighton. He entered many football fans' lives very briefly in the late 1980s when he tried, and failed, to buy Manchester United. He re-entered my life on Sunday 17 May 1992. We had just finished rock bottom of the entire Football League, saved from non-League football by the demise of some southern colleagues, and at the time I was a student in Nottingham. As was the norm for the weekends, my parents phoned on the Sunday and, unusually, my dad was very keen to speak to me as soon as he could.

–'Have you seen the paper?' he asked.

I replied that I hadn't.

–'Remember that bloke who juggled the ball at Old Trafford when he went to buy Man U?'

–'Yes.' I was frantically searching for a point in all of this.

–'Well he's bought Carlisle. It's in your brother's paper.'

And so he had.

The Carlisle local paper, *The Evening News and Star*, greeted the news the next day with the headline 'MR MONEYBAGS BUYS UNITED'. Knighton, the archetypal 'flamboyant' character, came full of promises; Carlisle were to be in the top flight within ten years and a force to be reckoned with. But with the benefit of hindsight for eight of those years, this promise rings as hollow as many of the others Knighton was to make. The 'Carlisle Gateway Millennium Project', a showpiece stadium development incorporating a hotel, golf course and lake for watersports and wildlife, amounted to little more than new East Stand – sixteen metres too long, and a project for which Carlisle has been paying interest to Knighton Holdings for longer than we care to remember. Peter Beardsley has never arrived at Brunton Park, despite endless rumours. Carlisle have never (thank God) merged with Clydebank and taken a place in the Scottish League. Instead, Carlisle under Knighton have been treated to a

From Old Trafford to Brunton Park – Michael Knighton. (Photo: News and Star.)

rollercoaster ride of epic proportions, and one which very nearly dipped out into the Vauxhall Conference.

The manager, Aidan MacCaffery, was the first casualty of the Knighton era in 1992/93. His replacement was shuffled aside after less than a year for the new director of coaching, Mick Wadsworth. The 1993/94 season saw a fantastic end to the campaign, which culminated in a play-off berth, and hopes were raised for the following year.

The 1994/95 season will go down as one of the most successful in the club's history. Runaway champions of Division Three, a club record unbeaten run of 19 games in the League and a first ever Wembley appearance were just some of the highlights of the year. We constantly played excellent football and before we knew it, we were a Division Two side. Then the wheels fell off. The problem with winning everything in sight by so much was that the coaching staff, board and fans all thought we were good enough for the higher division. For whatever reason, and largely it had to do with a spanking new stand which needed to be paid for, we found ourselves back in the familiar position of the basement division.

Not being a club that believes in consolidation, we bounced back. New manager Mervyn Day took us back to Wembley, where we won this time, and took us back to Division Two. Then, only a handful of games into the Division Two season, he was sacked and the chairman took over. Oh dear. From that day we were relegated – it was just that the maths needed to be confirmed. That didn't take all that long and we all sat and contemplated how a man such as Knighton, who had achieved hero status in 1995, could now become a villain to us.

The 1998/99 season started without the optimism of the previous years. Back in Division Three was not what we had hoped for and although we all spoke of bouncing straight back, very few genuinely believed it. The coaching was being shared between the youth team coach (to the point at which the youth team was virtually disbanded), the football in the community officer and the chairman. It looked like 'consolidation' would be classed as a successful year. It started reasonably. Hull were awful and laid an early claim to ninety-second place. Hartlepool and Scarborough joined in and we generally hung around the bottom half of the table annoying nobody.

Manager Nigel Pearson.
(Photo: News and Star.)

Then things took a turn for the worse. Hull hit form and Scarborough and Hartlepool began to pick up points while we found the sort of consistency that gives fans cardiac problems. The bottom of the League began to rise up towards us. Nigel Pearson was appointed manager and two of the Holy Trinity were removed for the club (surprisingly, the chairman did not sack himself from all affiliation). Winter began to turn to spring and we continued to lose with regularity that All Bran would love to lay claim to.

The unthinkable was not mentioned but slowly, in much the same way as I imagine a lioness stalks its prey, the drop-zone lurked, barely seen, in the background until eventually it pounced. And once it attacked it didn't want to let go. The next significant twist came on transfer deadline day. In all my years following Carlisle, this particular event has nearly always passed without comment. We never buy, or even loan, anyone of particular note at this time and so I suppose apathy has kicked in. It wasn't until much later that night, while idly flicking through Ceefax, that I noticed what had happened. We had sold our goalkeeper. Our only goalkeeper.

It's worth starting a new paragraph here and thinking about that for a moment. Carlisle United, a club who were in the middle of the most fundamental relegation battle of them all had sold the one and only recognised goalkeeper at the club. I see. Not only that, but we sold him for £5,000 to a club at the lower reaches of the Division Two. You can't really believe it, can you? I'll re-cap once more. Carlisle, a club that had made a £1.4 million profit the previous season (a relegation campaign), substantially more than several Premiership clubs, had sold their only goalkeeper on transfer deadline day because he would be available for a free transfer at the end of the season and had suggested that he would leave. The club thought it would be better to have the £5,000 in the bank rather than stay in League, or at least that is how it felt.

To help alleviate the pain a new 'keeper was brought in, on the same transfer deadline day, to help us see through to the end of the season. The official announcement made it clear that he was a Premiership goalie. Premiership in the sense that his contract was held by a Premiership club and not in the sense that he had ever turned out for said Premiership club. Derby County felt that, with a handful of games left and with little for themselves to play for, they could probably do without their third choice stopper for a while and so Richard Knight found himself thrown into a League survival battle. Well, it would be good experience for the lad.

Knight came and played. He saved a few. He let a couple in. Nobody was going to blame him if we got relegated, but it was unlikely that he was going to save us either. Except that he did – well in a manner. With three games left for United, one of Derby's 'keepers got injured and, presumably, Jim Smith phoned Brunton Park.

–'Just thought I'd call to see how my lad was doing.'

Sir Jimmy of Carlisle. (Photo: News and Star.)

–'Fine. Thanks again for the help, Jim.'

–'Aye, no problem. Except that I need him back. One of my other 'keepers is taking up space on the physio's table and Premiership rules say I must have a goalkeeper amongst my subs. I'll pay for his bus fare back you can tell him.'

And so Carlisle were once more goalkeeper-less.

Aside from the rules stating that you must play a goalkeeper, there is of course a very good footballing reason for a side needing to win its final games to have a goalie. So Carlisle approached the Football League and told them of their misfortune. The League granted United special dispensation to get another 'keeper on loan.

Enter, then, over the hills on a white steed, one Sir James Glass. Having just lost to Scarborough in a definite six-pointer, Carlisle's position looked bad. So bad indeed that Jimmy Glass said after the events of 8 May that if he had realised the predicament that Carlisle were in, he probably wouldn't have come. However, Carlisle still stood one place off the bottom of the pile with a game to play, while Scarborough were two points behind with a game in hand.

The game in hand was against Plymouth, the side Carlisle would face on the final day. The 3-0 victory which Scarborough pulled off over the South West side was quite a shock. Suddenly, as the final day approached, Carlisle found themselves ninety-second for the first time that season with only one game to play. The morning of Saturday 8 May 1999 dawned.

All Carlisle fans spent a lot of time looking at the table in the week preceding the game, but for no real reason as the maths was very simple. We had to do one better than Scarborough. If they drew, we had to win, but if they won – well, there was nothing we could do about rescuing ourselves if that happened. The local press ran an excellent campaign to urge people to attend the game. Wherever you went in the city, football was on everyone's lips for the first time since the 1997 Wembley trip.

My memory of the build-up to the game is hazy. I was nervous and was building myself up to a disappointment that I knew I couldn't even begin to imagine. I repeatedly told myself that if the worst happened I could say that I was at Carlisle's last League game, but, unsurprisingly, this didn't help one iota.

I was shocked when I got to Brunton Park. All season I had strolled in at about 2.50 p.m. and stood, with an untainted view, where I always did. Today, although not full, a healthy crowd had gathered. Many had come to cheer on the lads and do their bit. Many had been attracted by the vulture syndrome. Some were probably lost.

The game started with a let-down. As a rule I don't buy programmes, but today was special and so I decided to make an exception. Or at least I would have if they hadn't sold out. So I wandered into the Paddock terraced area and met up with some work colleagues. I stood, braced myself, tuned my personal stereo to BBC Radio Cumbria and, hands firmly in pockets, began to pray.

The first half was dire. The players were nervous. The crowd were worse. It was almost as if the tension on the terraces and in the stands was creating some sort of magnetic field that stopped passes finding their man or shots their target. In truth, and with the benefit of hindsight, I can now remind myself that I was watching one poor side (Plymouth) and one bloody awful side (Carlisle). But then, a moment of joy and excitement. The only pity is that it happened a couple of hundred miles away on the East Coast.

The radio informed me that Scarborough were losing. I shouted this information to anyone within earshot. The same was happening all around the ground. On the tape of the Radio Cumbria commentary you can hear the buzz circle the ground. It took the players only a few seconds to get the drift and, for a few brief moments, both the crowd and the team raised their game. Half time soon approached and the mood once more changed. The radio let us know of a Scarborough equaliser and we entered the break just as we had started forty-five minutes before.

The atmosphere during the interval was the most surreal experience that I have ever encountered at a football ground. The crowd divided into small huddles of people. Some pockets were the gloom and doom merchants, some could see how the winning goal was going to come (or so they thought), while some spoke of anything but the football. If I'm honest I can't remember which of the categories I fell into. But I can remember what it felt like when Plymouth scored.

A couple of minutes before the goal we were given a warning. Lee Phillips of Plymouth broke down the right unchallenged and attempted a shot. It wasn't the best strike of the ball and Glass saved. About ninety seconds later we got an action replay except this time Jimmy had to pick the ball out of the net. We could only imagine the scenes at Scarborough when this news filtered through and, whereas a few seconds before we had been one solitary goal from survival, now we were two and we only had 41 minutes to get them in.

The goal was a real shot in the arm for the crowd. Everyone was on their feet and behind the side. For a couple of minutes, one or two heads dropped both on and off the field, but these were picked up by the noise that the 7,000 Cumbrians were creating. For the first time in the entire game Carlisle played like the angry, wounded beast that we all thought we should have been, but still you couldn't see where a goal was coming from. In the end it came from the second least likely source.

During a little spell of pressure the ball was headed out of the Plymouth area. It fell to David Brightwell, Carlisle's honest if not gifted captain, about thirty yards out. He shaped to volley. Ordinarily he would have missed it completely or sent it out for a throw-in on the opposite side of the pitch. On this occasion, however, God (always one for the dramatic finish) let Brightwell strike the ball as he never has before or is unlikely ever to again. It whistled into the net. In an ordinary season the goal would have won countless plaudits among Cumbrians, but it was to be overshadowed a little later.

The celebrations by players, coaches and the fans were workman-like. Applause, pats on the back and the screaming of encouragement. I heard myself shout 'One more! One more lads' and must have looked at my watch a thousand times. Half an hour to go. The next thing I remember is confirmation of the final whistle at the McChip Stadium and the fourth official holding up a four to tell us how long we had to play.

It was hell to be at Brunton Park for those four minutes; it must have been just as bad at Scarborough. The second hand of my watch raced around at several times the speed it usually did. A spell of pressure led to a corner. A look at my watch suggested time was up. With nothing to lose we screamed at our goalkeeper to go and join the attack. He looked at the bench and Nigel Pearson waved him forward. Before I go any further, bear this thought in mind: in the previous forty-five league games that season we had scored a grand total of no goals directly as a result of a corner. Keep that thought for a moment.

Graham Anthony waited as Jimmy Glass sprinted up-field. We later found out that Brightwell had asked the referee how long was left, to be told 'Ten seconds. This is your last chance, son.' As soon as Graham Anthony took the corner I thought we had scored. Scott Dobie rose and headed the ball goalward. The 'keeper made a stunning reflex save and the chance seemed, in that split second, to have gone. But no! The ball fell at the feet of the red shirt with the big white number one on it. Next thing I knew I was in the air, arms waving wildly and with my throat becoming rapidly more and more hoarse. We'd only gone and bloody well nicked it.

When things began to calm down, the sight I was greeted with was of a pitch full of supporters with, amongst the throng, the ten blue and one red shirts of the team striving to get back into their own half so that we could play out the remainder of what little time was left. After

On-loan goalkeeper Jimmy Glass scores to keep Carlisle in the League. (Photo: News and Star.)

Jubilant fans after the Plymouth game. (Photo: News and Star.)

several minutes the players were in position, Glass back in his goal, and the fans back on the correct side of the advertising hoardings. The referee blew his whistle. The Plymouth players kicked off and the referee gave two shrill blasts. The game was over and we had, somehow, survived. The pitch filled with bodies and the players were carried off shoulder high.

My over-riding memory of the moment our remarkable journey ended is the feeling of pure relief and joy. All around me people were singing, cheering and embracing. In the distance I saw a friend of mine run onto the pitch. I followed and we stood on the turf slapping each other on the back as if trying to wake the other up from what must surely have been a dream.

The team were paraded in the director's box as if we had won the European Cup. Each one, regardless of their performance that day or throughout the season, was cheered and revered. And then Jimmy stepped forward. The entire ground erupted. I will never forget that moment. Eventually the time to depart came and I left the remaining masses who continued the party. On the way back to the car I caught up with two guys wearing the green and white of Argyle. They raved about what they had just witnessed, almost as excited as the United fans who had shared the experience with them. As we parted we shook hands and wished each other the best of luck for the next year.

Over the summer much changed and it was vowed that the mistakes of 1998/99 would not be repeated. Jimmy Glass returned to Swindon. His record of played three, scored one was significantly better than many strikers I have seen play for United. Nigel Pearson didn't have his contract renewed and Keith Mincher was appointed head coach. He held the post for five days and then remembered that he already had a job in the USA and that the commute for training would be a problem. Martin Wilkinson was given the job and he, in his other role of general manager, succeeded in passing it onto various other odd-bods during the season, although it kept coming back to him. The net result – we found ourselves in the middle of a relegation battle once more, and, once more, the last day of the season was to decide our fate and our League future. We had been promised it would never happen again – and twelve months later it duly did.

Things were more complicated this time. If we beat Brighton we

Carlisle battle for survival against Brighton. (Photo: News and Star.)

It doesn't get any better than this! (Photo: News and Star.)

were safe, if Peterborough beat Chester we were safe, but various different combinations could mean either ourselves, Shrewsbury or Chester could face the drop. First Shrewsbury took a two-goal lead – no matter, that didn't affect us. Then, in a moment of abject horror, Brighton scored. Ninety-second place was ours. Fortunately, Peterborough had read the script, and soon after news filtered through from Chester that they had taken the lead. I screamed and punched the air.

The scores at Chester and Brighton remained the same and we survived once more. Except this time there was no glorious party, no story to tell. Only questions of how on earth were we here again?

And now? Eleven games into the 2000/01 season we are third off bottom, without a home win and, as I write, in the worst run of straight defeats the club has had since William the Conqueror was sacked for leaving the club out of the Rothmans Doomsday Book. Knighton has officially left. I say officially as he has resigned as chairman (again) and a new one has been appointed. He has also been disqualified from being a company director for five-and-a-half years by the DTI (it's a long story). He is still involved a little, however, as he owns a small portion of the club's shares – 93 per cent of them to be exact. The current board are trying to buy him out but appear to lack the necessary funds.

New manager Ian Atkins (who almost saved Chester from relegation last year in a wicked twist of irony) is working with a budget of less than nothing and the new squad is almost entirely made up of loan signings, free transfers and trialists. Most of players would consider a three-month contract as a long-term deal and many are on month-to-month.

This year's team, to be fair to them, have shown much more spirit and fight than last year's collection, but you don't get points for that. This looks as if it will be another long, hard season, but in Atkins we have, for the first time in many years, a manager who knows what he is doing and who can motivate a team. If a few results go our way, who knows what will happen. If they don't, we all know what will happen.

Still, never a dull moment.

Fans celebrate a second last-day escape in two years. (Photo: News and Star.)

American Dream, British Nightmare (Chester City)

Paul Grech

1999/2000   Bottom of Division Three and relegated to the Conference
2000/01   Eighth in Conference

The American Dream is the ideal that anyone with enough vision and enough will-power can overcome the odds to achieve unhoped-for results and success. The mentality that has pushed Americans to achieve great results in almost every field of modern society and which in turn has bred an in-built belief among Americans that they are the best at everything.

Most probably, it is this mentality that led American Terry Smith into taking over Chester City. If he was looking for a club where he could be the architect of a rags-to-riches story, then he couldn't have made a better choice.

For two years, Chester had been operating under the constant threat of being closed down after being placed in administration. When the club's owner, Mark Guterman, decided to sell his majority shareholding, it was only through the joint efforts of the Independent Supporters Association and manager Kevin Ratcliffe that the club stayed afloat. Formed in 1998 by six devoted fans, the ISA soon became a conduit of ideas between the club, their supporters and the community. They embarked on a leaflet campaign aimed at increasing awareness of the club's plight. The campaign turned out to be a huge success with attendances at the Deva Stadium nearly doubling and money being raised to pay some of the club's creditors. As events at the club unravelled, the ISA would take an increasingly more important role.

On the pitch, Kevin Ratcliffe performed miracles. Forced to survive without having any money to spend, and constantly having to sell his best players in order to bring in some much-needed cash, the former Everton and Wales man somehow managed to keep the club in the Football League. Like the fans, he was passionate about the team which had given him his first chance in football, so much so that on one occasion he forked out £5,000 of his own money to pay the local water board after supply had been switched off due to mounting debts.

During this period, a number of prospective buyers turned up, including a consortium led by David Pickering which made a serious offer for the club. This bid was, however, based on the plan of closing down the club – hence clearing the £500,000 owed to various creditors – and then forming a 'phoenix' company. Justifiably, the Football League rejected this idea.

So Chester lurched from one deadline to another until, with the start of the 1999/2000 season a matter of weeks away, the Football League announced that no club under administration would be allowed to start the new campaign. It was at this point that Terry Smith entered the scene like the proverbial knight in shining armour. The sequence of events which led him to take over the club is the stuff of fairy tales. Originally attracted to the local zoo, which he often visited with his young daughters, the former Manchester Spartans and Great Britain American football coach heard of the financial problems being faced by the local football club. Backed by his Florida-based millionaire father, he made a bid for the club and late in June

Terry Smith: he visited a zoo and bought a football club. (Photo: Dale Miles.)

1999 became the new owner of Chester City.

Fearful that their team might go the same way as Aldershot or Newport, the Chester supporters breathed a collective sigh of relief. At last, here was a man who was willing to plough part of his apparently considerable fortune into their team. The initial signs were promising, especially when Smith agreed to allow three members of the ISA into the board of directors. Smith's initial comments also hit the right notes. First he assured Ratcliffe of his job, then spoke about his plans. 'I do have contacts from the American Soccer League and American internationals and internationals from the EEC countries coming to Chester is a possibility.' To back this claim, Icelandic winger Petur Jonnson was among the 6,000 strong crowd at the Deva Stadium that witnessed a close 3-2 defeat by neighbouring Everton in Smith's first match as chairman.

Unfortunately, the honeymoon period was soon cut short. Three games into the new season, Kevin Ratcliffe, the man who lived and breathed Chester and who had forked money out of his own pocket to help the club, suddenly resigned. The first signs of trouble had appeared a couple of weeks earlier when it was reported that some players were unhappy at only being granted short term contracts. Smith replied, 'There is absolutely no reason for this doom and gloom attitude. Any player who has left can be replaced, and each will be replaced with a new player who will be of exceptional standard.' But a few days later, defender and skipper Andy Crosby left for Brighton & Hove Albion with the parting shot that the club was 'falling apart'.

It was in these strained circumstances that Ratcliffe started the new season and, with the smallest squad in the Football League under his charge, it was little wonder that the first three games all ended in defeat. Still, his sudden resignation came as a surprise, as was Smith's explanation for Ratcliffe's actions, 'Kevin didn't want to be associated with a club at the bottom of the League. It wasn't good for his career.'

Ratcliffe, however, offered a different version of the facts – one where the main reason for his departure was Smith himself. 'It's the American thing. Nice to your face, picking your brains and all that, then he casts you aside. He'd never played the game, he'd very rarely even been to see a match. Yet he was selling and buying players behind my back. Every day I turned up for training there were trialists left on my doorstep, kids who were taken on simply because they had written or phoned the club without any background whatsoever in football.'

Later on in the season, Ratcliffe took over at fellow Third Division strugglers Shrewsbury, but Chester still had to pay £200,000 in compensation according to a clause in Ratcliffe's contract which entitled him to a severance payment should he leave the Deva when a new owner came in. Smith professed that, somewhat naively, he hadn't seen Ratcliffe's contract before taking over the club and initially refused to pay the amount, but was forced to do so by a tribunal.

If Ratcliffe's resignation and the subsequent discovery of the clause in his contract surprised the Chester faithful, the next developments left them speechless. Instead of naming a new manager, Terry Smith announced that the team would be led by a five-man coaching squad formed by David Fogg, Gary Shelton, Shaun Reid, Scott Cooper and Smith himself. Even more astonishingly, for a man who had rarely been to a football match, Smith was confident enough to install himself as the club's head coach. One anecdote which highlights Smith's lack of knowledge about the game is told by Ian Atkins, the man who would later take charge of the team. 'The American owner, Terry Smith, had coached the side and we were talking tactics one day. "Jeez," he said, "I never read that in the book"'.

This lack of knowledge mattered little to Smith. He had hinted at his desire to be involved in the running of the side upon buying the club. Smith's confidence was also borne out by the fact that he had been a successful coach in the Americans' version of football. As head coach with the Manchester Spartans he had handled every aspect of team administration and had won the European Championship before going on to coach the Great Britain team. As a result of his successes he was named Great Britain and European Coach of the Year. During his time as Chester manager, he would claim that 'No one else connected with Chester City Football Club has ever won a European Championship.'

Whatever the reason, Smith saw himself fit enough to manage Chester City and started by appointing three departmental captains: Ross Davidson was appointed to captain the defence, Nick Richardson the midfield and Luke Beckett the attack. Such tactics are commonplace in American football where a different set of players take to the field according to whether the team is attacking or defending. As such, 'zonal' captains are needed to marshal the different sets of players. In football, bar the three possible substitutions, the same players remain on the pitch for the whole ninety minutes, making 'zonal' captains superfluous and, most probably, confusing for the players involved. It is also difficult to imagine the typical British player being impressed by the seven-page motivation dossiers that Smith handed out before games in order to pump up his players.

Despite the general scepticism, Smith remained defensive of his methods. In one interview, he claimed 'I do not agree that they didn't work. With zonal captains, I was simply giving the individual players more responsibility. I can tell you that when I took over, the players said I gave them a new impetus and that under the old regime they were not learning anything in training. It is easy to look at results and say that there has been no progress.'

But in football, as in any other competitive sport, it is the results that count. In 22 games under Smith's leadership, Chester collected only 16 points, coming from four wins and four draws, and conceded 44 goals.

Ian Atkins, Chester manager. (Photo: Dale Miles.)

After two heavy back-to-back defeats by two teams also fighting to avoid the drop, 5-1 to Leyton Orient and 4-1 to Carlisle, the respected Ian Atkins was appointed to take over the team.

Atkins' appointment was, however, preceded by a scathing attack by the club towards the local media, an attack probably instigated by Smith, whose mistrust of the media had reached considerable proportions. In a statement claiming that Chester had been damaged in its efforts to appoint a new manager due to the 'false media reporting', the club pointed a blaming finger towards the media: 'Chester City wants to state that the club has repeatedly asked for all the doom and gloom negative reporting from many members of the media that have covered the club this season to stop. However, the media have refused to stop such pessimistic attitudes and this negativity has contributed greatly to the difficult League position that the club finds itself in.'

Although it is difficult to fathom how any media reporting, irrespective of its negativity, could be the reason for a club losing most of its matches, it is slightly easier to understand Smith's diffident view. On one radio programme, Radio Five's *On the Line*, his past achievements in American football were put in doubt when it was claimed that Smith's experience with the New England Patriots NFL team amounted to two pre-season friendlies before injuries forced him to quit. His background made him an easy target and at one time he almost pleadingly claimed: 'All I ever asked was to be judged in the same way as an English coach would have been judged, given the budget within which we had to operate.'

Significantly, however, Atkins was appointed as director of football with the press release announcing his appointment stressing that 'the board of Chester City has made the decision to leave Smith as manager and leave the rest of the coaching staff in place because they feel that now is not the time to wipe the slate clean.'

Director of football or not, it was Atkins who led the side for the rest of the season. He brought in twelve new players, mostly experienced professionals, and despite a 7-1 defeat at the hands of Brighton & Hove Albion – the heaviest home defeat in the club's history – was close to completing the virtually impossible job of saving the club. In the end, a 1-0 home defeat by Peterborough condemned Chester to non-League football as the club agonisingly finished bottom on goal difference.

Optimistic Chester fans before the crunch game against Peterborough. (Photo: Dale Miles.)

Carl Heggs and Luke Beckett fail to convert against the Posh. (Photo: Dale Miles.)

Immediately after the relegation, the recriminations started. The ISA summed up the fans' anger when it blamed Smith for most of the club's problems, including the resignations of Ratcliffe and other key staff like David Fogg, and accused him of economising on player signings instead of bringing in the promised 'top foreign players'.

Fogg's resignation didn't go down too well with Smith, particularly after he joined Ratcliffe at Shrewsbury Town. Smith lodged a complaint over an illegal approach with the Football League in which he demanded that Shrewsbury be docked three points – thus re-instating Chester in Division Three – and pay compensation of around £1 million. As a supporters' club spokesman said, 'it is making the club a laughing stock.' The Football League agreed and, after reprimanding Shrewsbury, asked both clubs to pay the costs for the case.

Smith would astonishingly also launch an attack on Ian Atkins saying that the 23 points obtained in 21 games were 'unsatisfactory'. He also claimed that 'The club has spent massive amounts of money signing twelve players since January, doubling the wage bill' – an indirect criticism of Atkins' transfer policy. For Atkins this was probably the straw that broke the camel's back. Having initially commented 'if a plan is put in place, I'd love to stay' he subsequently opted to join Carlisle. Later on, he'd reply to Smith's comments: 'I've kept quiet because I didn't want to rock the boat. All he (Smith) ever wanted to do was to manage the team again. He wanted to do it all himself, yet when I arrived I found a team in complete disarray. His hair style makes him look like Coco the Clown and at times I'm afraid that he has acted like a clown. The reason the club finds itself in the Conference is down to him.'

Atkins' decision to leave further angered the fans and Smith continued to lose his grip on the situation when two of the three members the ISA elected among the board of directors resigned within weeks of each other. One, Paul Murray, explicitly stated that his decision to leave was due to a 'difference of opinion with the chairman.' The third member elected on the board would follow suit a couple of months later.

Faced by a mass player exodus, led by leading scorer Luke Beckett, Smith finally made a popular decision by appointing Graham Barrow as the new manager. Having played over 200 games for City, Barrow was the manager who had led the club to promotion to the Second Division in 1994, an

Tensions run high – Chester versus Peterborough, 6 May 2000. (Photo: Dale Miles.)

achievement fondly remembered by the fans. However, Smith would soon erase any positive effect that Barrow's appointment might have had by backtracking on a promise to drop admission prices, a knee-jerk reaction to the club's relegation. Having previously commented that the club was in its best financial position for many years, most fans were understandably annoyed when Smith stated that the club's dire financial position was the reason for the highest admission prices in the league.

And the trouble was not over for Smith. Harry McNally, appointed the club's chief scout, resigned two weeks into the job, claiming 'I have been in professional football for over forty years but working with Mr Smith for a week was more than enough'. Nor was this the last resignation. Three months into the new season, two chiefs of security had resigned and on one occasion this forced the postponement of a match, earning the club a hefty fine.

Then, out of the blue, came the news that most Chester fans had been waiting for. Terry Smith announced that he was putting the club up for sale, claiming that over-work was stressing him out and preventing him from spending enough time with his children. For all his misguided leadership, it is undeniable that Terry Smith saved Chester City from extinction and has reportedly cleared all of the club's debt, for which the fans should be grateful. It has also been reported that he is only interested in selling the club to Chester supporters and that he wants the next owner to be someone who secures the future of the club. Whether that happens when push comes to the shove remains to be seen, especially since the name of Mark Guterman, the club's previous owner and the man who put Chester in the hands of the receiver, is once again being mentioned.

Despite everything, there remains real hope about Chester's future. As one judge claimed after turning down a winding-up order, 'there is a genuine prospect of success but somebody has to come forward with new money.' Over the past couple of years, the ISA have proved beyond all doubt that, despite being dwarfed by the neighbouring Liverpool and Everton, when an effort is made, the supporters will turn up at the Deva Stadium.

The stadium itself is the club's main asset and at least the fans don't have to worry that any owner will buy the club to strip it of that asset, as happened at Brighton. The stadium is leased to the club by the local council and it is certain that any efforts to buy the lease will be turned down. Still, the club and its fans had to pay a high price for the Deva, being forced into exile for two years at the start of the 1990s. Many point at those couple of seasons as the start of Chester's troubles. Home attendances, if you could call them that seeing that home matches were played at Macclesfield's Moss Road, fell to an average of slightly above 1,000. A whole generation of supporters was lost and the financial burden of building the ground meant that few resources could go towards

Despair at the final whistle. (Photo: Chester Evening Reader.)

strengthening the team, even when the stadium was built. When the side gained promotion to the Second Division in 1994, financial resources were so scarce that the club couldn't afford to offer the players new contracts.

In order to survive, the club had to sell and one of those to go was midfielder Matt McKay, who joined Everton for £250,000 (which could rise to £750,000 according to appearances). McKay had made his debut for Chester at the age of seventeen and was a product of Chester's other principal asset, their youth policy. Among the few to save themselves from the relegation season were youngsters like Darren Moss and Darren Wright. Like McKay, they will most probably be snapped up by clubs further up the hierarchy, but with such young players coming through lies much of Chester's hope for the future.

For now, that future lies in the hands of Terry Smith, although for how long remains to be seen. Despite all the problems, Chester started their first season in the non-League well, but the lack of stability at the club will certainly leave its mark.

The Conference is a difficult league to get out of, as Hereford, Doncaster and Scarborough have found out in recent seasons. Most of the clubs in the division know what it takes to compete at this level and, more importantly, what it takes to run a club efficiently at this level. But for Chester, this is a new experience and it will take time to adjust; but for the club's American owner, the strain of this adjustment period has proved to be too much.

At one point, Smith stated 'I want to feel I've done something important for those generations who have followed this club so that their memories will be saved.' Ironically, even though he may have saved the club from extinction, it is doubtful whether he will be remembered fondly by most supporters. Terry Smith may have embarked on the Chester City adventure in the hope of fulfilling the American Dream but, in the end, it has turned out to be a nightmare.

A bitter pill. (Photo: Chester Evening Reader.)

CONTRIBUTORS

Ian Anderson is twenty-two-year-old student at Coventry University, where his masochistic streak (previously only shown in his choice of football team to support) manifested itself in his decision to study economics and German. Hailing from the less-than-glamorous seaside town of Bridlington in East Yorkshire, Ian has been a Scarborough fan since the age of twelve and, whilst he cannot make every home game due to his current location, he has been a regular contributor to various Boro fanzines in the past.

Roy Chuter isn't sure what he does for a living, but it involves writing about football and coming up with new ways of looking at the game. He regards supporting Brighton & Hove Albion as a compulsory part of his life – his family has followed the club since it was formed 100 years ago. By the time he was old enough to wonder why, he was hooked for life.

Anthony Donnelly is a twenty-nine-year-old production manager who has spent the last ten years of his life caring too much about Carlisle United. After first experiencing United in the glorious Peter Beardsley era, they left his life until he went to university, where supporting one of the worst football clubs in the country struck him as a good way to get people to like him. Anthony now lives in Doncaster with his wife and two children and is proud that the last goal he saw as a resident of Carlisle was the infamous Jimmy Glass injury-time winner. The best player he has seen in a Carlisle United shirt is Peter Beardsley and his ambition for the club is for them to have a boring mid-table season in the Football League.

Doug Embleton is managing director of his own company, The Language Service Limited, which he established in 1994 after his own equivalent of relegation to the Conference ... redundancy. He is a Fellow of the Institute of Translation and Interpreting and also a Fellow of the Institute of Linguists. Doug is also an avid fan of Darlington FC (which frequently features in the company's newsletter) as well as being a collector of rock 'n' roll records for his jukeboxes.

Bob Gilbert is old enough to remember the good times at his beloved Doncaster Rovers. From his dad's shoulders he watched a 10-0 win over Darlington and later, AWOL from university, he saw the Rovers reach the quarter-finals of the then League Cup. He's seen them play at Anfield, St James Park and Goodison and he saw them beat the then First Division QPR in the FA Cup. Now he watches them at Hednesford, Forest Green and Hayes. Still, Bob is not despondent. Having played a significant role in the campaign to rid the Rovers of Ken Richardson, about whom the Doncaster chapter is devoted, he has seen with his own eyes that Conference football is undoubtedly as good as the Third Division, that you can buy a pint inside most Conference grounds and that the opposition supporters are a pretty decent bunch. Bob is a Rovers exile, having lived in Gloucestershire for many years, but he is continuing to play a role within the Rovers supporters' community through his involvement in the creation of a Rovers Trust designed to help the club on its path to recovery. He is, however, currently engaged in a fierce debate with his partner about just which team the expected new arrival will support. His partner is a committed Reading supporter (... better than Man Utd though). Bob would like to dedicate this chapter to both this new arrival and to his late father, Ray Gilbert, who died suddenly shortly after the successful conclusion of his even more passionate and articulate defence of the Rovers.

For most Liverpool fans, Chester City is simply the club from whom they bought Ian Rush in the early 1980s. Those more interested in trivia will also tell you that Chester is the birthplace of Michael Owen. But twenty-four-year-old Liverpool fan **Paul Grech** got interested in Chester City after reading an article about their American owner and started following their situation with increasing interest, writing a number of articles in order to raise some awareness about their plight. Maltese-born Paul is the articles editor at www.footie51.co.uk, apart from being sports editor at the Maltese weekly newspaper Il-Gens and contributor to various other publications.

Andrew Hodson combines working at the family firm, Acewell Electronics Ltd with a passion for the beautiful game, first as a player and then a supporter of Burnley. At twenty-nine, Andrew is now approaching the peak of his footballing ability. As a devastatingly quick and powerful striker, he is often found lurking just outside the immediate danger area, although a recent move into a role just behind the front man has allowed him to roam more dangerously out of position. Five-a-side has allowed him to turn over Saturdays to watching his beloved Burnley, a task he has undertaken since the late 1970s. Although only sixteen years old when the Clarets reached their lowest ebb against Orient, the memory is still vivid and he hopes to be watching Burnley in the Premiership before long.

Matt Hudson is twenty-three, and is chief of media for Division Two side Colchester United. Having grown up in the area and followed the U's since he was ten, this is a dream job for Matt, and his main responsibility will be to develop the club's website. (http://www.colchesterunited.net). Prior to working for Colchester, Matt was a journalist for leading website Football365.

Johnny Meynell has been following the fortunes of Halifax Town for over twenty-one years and has been a regular contributor to the matchday programme. In 1999 he had his first book published, entitled *Halifax Town: From Ball To Lillis*. He has worked for Calderdale Council since 1981 and is currently employed as a mobile library supervisor. Though now aged thirty-seven, he still somehow manages to get out of bed on a Sunday morning and turn out for Halifax Rangers (Reserves) in the Halifax Sunday League, and also plays five-a-side on most of the other days of the week. Married to Denise, he has a two-year-old daughter, Samantha.

Ron Parrott was born in 1950 and has been a lifelong supporter of Hereford United, following in the footsteps of his grandfather, who was chairman of the Supporters' Club and sports reporter for the Hereford Times from the 1920s through till the early '60s. Ron has in the past run the club shop at Edgar Street and has recently written and published a book, *The League Era* on the twenty-five-year Football League history of Hereford United between 1972 and 1997. Ron still keeps himself fit, with twice-a-week circuit training and the occasional game of squash and five-a-side football, as well as pursuing his main passion of mountaineering. He is currently almost half-way towards completing the 284 Scottish 'Munros' (mountains over 3,000 feet in height).

At the age of twenty-eight, **George Rowland** is close to accepting that he may not have a career as a professional footballer. With a spare million pounds at his disposal he would happily donate the sum to a struggling club, provided that, in exchange, he was allowed to have his ten minutes of glory as a substitute in an unimportant, end-of-season, mid-table fixture. Failing that, he will probably have to settle for writing football books. *The Ultimate Drop* is his second, following *If the Titanic had been Sky Blue*, a work on his beloved Coventry City. When real life forces its ugly head in the way of football, he works as a nurse for people with learning disabilities. He is married to Caroline, and has two beautiful children – Lauren and Amy.

Tony Scholes is forty-eight years old and has worked in IT for the last twenty-five years. He has been supporting Burnley since 1960 (just a few months too late to see the Championship won, although he did see the European Cup games). The first game he saw was a 5-3 win against Manchester United. He was secretary of the Burnley Football Supporters' Club from 1983 to 1989, which of course included the fateful season of 1986/87. For the match against Colchester, when the attendance was the lowest since the Second World War, he was actually match ball sponsor. The period in the 1980s was difficult but he never lost his commitment, although going to games was sometimes a chore rather than a pleasure, and that commitment remains today. He is now heavily involved with the Clarets Independent Supporters' Association and is currently the membership secretary and also editor of the web site (www.burnleycisa.com).

Kevin Scott is a computer programming Essex boy who, despite living and working in various countries, has utterly failed to shake off his allegiance to Colchester United, having been frog-marched to watch them from an early age by his misguided family. He has often wondered why he couldn't have been born in Barcelona or Milan instead.

Neil Williams was born in February 1962 in Newport, and spent his first year of life within a goal kick of Somerton Park. His first ever game was Newport v. Hereford 1977, in which he decided to walk through the away following at half time to get a drink. You only do that sort of thing once! Having left school in 1978 to join the Army, following the County wasn't too difficult for the next two years as he was in training only fifteen miles away in Chepstow. After that it became more difficult as postings to Kent, Germany, Falklands, Canada, Yorkshire and the Gulf followed (you have to appreciate spending six months away at a location eight hours behind GMT to realise the importance of football, as you receive the Saturday results as you are getting up in the morning. Others have had all day to prepare themselves). In 1994 he left the

Army to become a police officer in Hampshire. It is deeply ironic that when a group of Newport supporters got together in 1996 to form an organisation for Newport supporters living across the border, it was held only half a mile away from where he lived in Basingstoke but he didn't know about it. He is now the editor for the newsletter of this organisation called *The Over The Bridge Exiles*, the membership of which is now over 100 (mostly in England, but with quite a few living as far away as Australia, New Zealand, Malaysia and America). This organisation, through its subscriptions and fund raising, have helped Newport County AFC to purchase players, equipment, and give donations as the need arises.

Igor Wowk was born in 1954 and went to his first League match at Peel Park, Accrington in the 1961/62 season. The second game he went to was Stanley's last win in the League in October 1961 against Crewe in front of 2,713 spectators. All the other Accrington fans are gradually dying off, so he is well on his way to being unique. Burnley were his second love; he went to watch them play Blackburn Rovers at Ewood near the end of the 1961/62 season when Burnley were on for the double. They lost to Blackburn twice, thus being prevented from winning the title and allowing Ipswich in to steal it; they lost the Cup Final to Spurs as well. Its been downhill ever since with the odd undulation. Igor went to school in Blackburn and in his first full season of organised football not only did he receive a winners medal as his side became Blackburn under-11s school champions, but he played at Ewood Park. However his playing career went downhill from then on and he was heartbroken when he wasn't selected for Blackburn Schoolboys (and thus knew he had virtually no chance of playing on Turf Moor). Subsequently he has done lots of boring jobs – i.e. not playing professional football, but nonetheless at forty-six he still plays five-a-side. Not only that, he got approached to play eleven-a-side last month, but the bloke had had a couple of pints at the time and hasn't seen him play recently (and it was an over-35s team). However, the motto still is 'Play till you drop. If you can't play, it's not worth getting up for anything else.'

Other football titles available from Tempus Publishing:

ISBN	Title	Author	Price
0 7524 2248 0	Accrington Stanley: Images	Phil Whalley	£10.99
0 7524 1862 9	Birmingham City: Images	Tony Matthews	£9.99
0 7524 2040 2	Bristol City 1894-1967: Images	Tom Hopegood	£9.99
0 7524 2249 9	Bristol City 1967-2001: Images	Tom Hopegood	£10.99
0 7524 1150 0	Bristol Rovers: Images	Mike Jay	£10.99
0 7524 1520 4	Burnley 1882-1968: Images	Ray Simpson	£10.99
0 7524 2256 1	Cambridge United : Images	Brian Attmore & Graham Nurse	£10.99
0 7524 2068 2	Cardiff City 1971-2000: Images	Richard Shepherd	£9.99
0 7524 1545 X	Crewe Alexandra : Images	Harold Finch	£9.99
0 7524 1544 1	Crystal Palace: Images	Revd Nigel Sands	£9.99
0 7524 2176 X	Crystal Palace: Greats	Revd Nigel Sands	£12.00
0 7524 1898 X	Devon Derbies	Mike Holgate	£12.99
0 7524 2189 1	Doncaster Rovers: Images	Peter Tuffrey	£10.99
0 7524 2259 6	Everton 1880-1945: Images	John Rowlands	£10.99
0 7524 1855 6	The Football Programme	John Litster	£12.99
0 7524 2042 9	Forever England	Mark Shaoul & Tony Williamson	£16.99
0 7524 1567 0	Gillingham: Images	Roger Triggs	£10.99
0 7524 2243 X	Gillingham: Men Who Made	Roger Triggs	£19.99
0 7524 1620 0	Hull City: Images	Chris Elton	£9.99
0 7524 2152 2	Ipswich Town: Images	Tony Garnett	£9.99
0 7524 1642 1	Leeds United: Images	David Saffer/Howard Dapin	£9.99
0 7524 2043 7	Leeds United in Europe	David Saffer	£9.99
0 7524 2094 1	Leyton Orient: Images	Neilson Kaufman	£9.99
0 7524 2255 3	Manchester City: Classics	Andrew Waldon	£12.00
0 7524 2085 2	Manchester City: Images	David Saffer & Andrew Waldon	£9.99
0 7524 1849 1	Millwall 1884-1939: Images	Millwall FC Museum	£9.99
0 7524 2187 5	Millwall 1940-2001: Images	Millwall FC Museum	£10.99
0 7524 2191 3	Motherwell: Men Who Made	Jim Jeffrey & Genge Fry	£15.00
0 7524 1081 4	Newport County 1912-1960: Images	Richard Shepherd	£10.99
0 7524 1671 5	Northampton Town: Images	John Watson & David Walden	£9.99
0 7524 1183 7	Oxford United: Images	Jon Murray	£9.99
0 7524 1185 3	Plymouth Argyle 1886-1986: Images	Gordon Sparks	£9.99
0 7524 1604 9	Queens Park Rangers: Images	Tony Williamson	£9.99
0 7524 1061 X	Reading 1871-1997: Images	David Downs	£10.99
0 7524 2081 X	Reading: Greats	David Downs	£12.00
0 7524 1063 6	Roker Park Voices	Alan Brett & Andrew Clark	£9.99
0 7524 1670 7	Rotherham United: Images	Gerry Somerton	£9.99
0 7524 1059 8	Sheffield United: Images	Denis Clarebrough	£9.99
0 7524 2264 2	Sheffield United: Greats	Denis Clarebrough	£12.00
0 7524 2089 5	Southend United: Images	Peter Miles& and Dave Goody	£9.99
0 7524 2177 8	Southend United: Greats	Peter Miles & Dave Goody	£12.00
0 7524 1698 7	Stoke City: Images	Tony Matthews	£9.99
0 7524 0716 3	Sunderland: Images	Alan Brett & George Hoare	£12.99
0 7524 1133 0	Swansea Town 1912-1964: Images	Richard Shepherd	£9.99
0 7524 2093 3	Swindon Town: Images	Richard Mattick	£9.99
0 7524 1814 9	Torquay United: Images	Mike Holgate	£9.99
0 7524 2044 5	Tottenham Hotspur 1882-1952: Images	Roy Brazier	£9.99
0 7524 1505 0	Tranmere Rovers: Images	Peter Bishop	£9.99
0 7524 1592 1	Vetch Field Voices	Keith Haynes	£9.99
0 7524 2091 7	Walsall: Images	Geoff Allman	£9.99
0 7524 2226 X	Wallsall: Greats	Geoff Allman	£12.00
0 7524 2056 9	West Brom Albion: Images	Tony Matthews	£9.99
0 7524 2224 3	West Brom Albion: Greats	Tony Matthews	£12.00
0 7524 2265 0	Wolverhampton Wanderers: Greats	Tony Matthews	£12.00
0 7524 2045 3	1966 World Cup	Norman Shiel	£9.99
0 7524 1899 8	Wrexham: Images	Gareth Davies & Peter Jones	£9.99
0 7524 1568 9	York City: Images	David Batters	£9.99